AF323358

CRESTED BUTTE STORIES... THROUGH MY LENS

CRESTED BUTTE STORIES...

THROUGH MY LENS

Sandra Cortner

WILD ROSE PRESS
Crested Butte, Colorado

ENDPAPERS: *front,* Elk Ave, 1982, first snow; *back,* cattle drive past the ski area, 1986
TITLE PAGE: Crested Butte Mountain emerges from a rainstorm in 1973.

Library of Congress Control Number 2006921153
ISBN 0-9777147-0-5

Printed in the United States of America
First printing May 2006
DESIGN BY JANE RAESE

Wild Rose Press
P.O. Box 203
Crested Butte, Colorado 81224

To Crested Butte's old-timers

ACKNOWLEDGMENTS

Many people helped to make this book a reality—first and foremost, the people of Crested Butte who turned their faces to me and entrusted me with their stories. I didn't set out to write a documented history but rather a collection of their tales and mine, from the heart, as accurately as we can remember them. I am deeply honored to have them speak through me.

Without Betty Barkman, who urged me to "create something for the joy of creation," this book would still be stories running around my head with a brain more interested in how to make money from it than how to make joy. With any luck I can make a little of both.

My writer's group has encouraged me through revision after revision: Betty, Barbara M. Crawford, Betsy Janney, Mike Keith, Bob Puglisi, and Sheila Davis. Special thanks to Marcie Telander for writing "Give me more!" on all my drafts and for inspiring me to dig deeper.

To my editors, both professional and amateur, including my clever sister-in-law Margie Payne, and my beloved husband, best critic, and editor, Greg Payne, for their support and advice—my deepest gratitude.

A special thanks to my family for wading through chapters and providing feedback, and especially to my sister Kathleen, who graciously allowed me to reconstruct our conversations and expose her to the reader.

Thank you to Paragon Computers and the Crested Butte Society, Inc. for technical support.

I am indebted to all the people whose brains I picked for obscure, almost forgotten facts, including Betty Spehar, Eleanor Stefanic, Frances Somrak, Trudy Yaklich, John Tezak Jr., Nick Rayder, Mary Jo Somrak, Mary Ann Fore, and George Sibley, along with so many others.

The Crested Butte Mountain Heritage Museum's display of all my old-timer photographs has helped to keep these people alive in our memories.

Thank you, all!

—*Sandra Cortner*
May 2006

CONTENTS

Prologue — ix

1   Crested Butte, 1964 . . . I Am Smitten — 1

2   Tony Mihelich and the Hardware — 21

3   Rip-Sawing Through the Fourth of July — 30

4   Rudy Sedmak — 40

5   Parenting a Newspaper — 58

6   If Stefanic's Don't Have It, You Don't Need It — 72

7   Memorial Day — 84

8   Hot and Cold—Heating with Wood, 1976–1989 — 91

9   Lyle's Freezer — 99

10   Flauschink Is Comink! — 108

11   Mushroom Fever — 117

12   The Kochevar Family — 125

13   From Trail to Table — 135

14   Play Ball! 1970–1985 — 142

15   Willard Ruggera — 150

16   Christmas in Crested Butte: 1980s Style — 159

17   Betty Spehar Grows Up — 166

18   Golden Marmots to Hollywood — 180

19   Grace Arnott — 191

20   Vinotok 1988, the Fall Wine Festival — 199

21   Frank Orazem's Walking Stick — 207

22   Angie's Garden — 211

23   Ms. Grubstake 1980 — 218

24   Mary Yelenick, the Weather Woman — 224

25   Buried in Paradise — 229

PROLOGUE

CRESTED BUTTE MOUNTAIN, poised like a lion on its haunches, its head a triangular crest, its mane the sheer cliffs flanked by groves of aspen and spruce, rises from a carpet of sagebrush and wildflowers.

Looming in the distance as you approach on Highway 135, it stands guard at the head of the verdant valley where its namesake town, Crested Butte, Colorado, is nestled in the heart of the Elk Mountains.

Rising above 12,000 feet, snowcapped peaks with names like Treasury, Ruby, Red Lady, and Cinnamon feed cascading streams that flow into the valley, where cattle graze on lush pastures of timothy grass. Fanning out from town, trails and four-wheel-drive roads lead to magical places: Oh-be-joyful Creek, Paradise Divide, Emerald Lake, and Pearl Pass.

European immigrants established Crested Butte in the 1880s. It became the railroad hub for surrounding mines and ranches. Long snowy winters at high elevation bred a community that was tough, resourceful, and self-reliant. Built of miners' cabins and Victorian structures, their small town would become a National Historic District, but not before being hit hard by the decline of the mining industry.

When I first arrived in Crested Butte in the summer of 1964, all I could see was what was on the surface: old houses with rusting roofs, empty unpaved streets, and crumbling concrete sidewalks. Its seven-square-block core was the size of my Tucson high school campus. My five-hundred member senior class, with whom I'd graduated two nights earlier, probably outnumbered the local population. The last of the region's coal mines on nearby Gibson Ridge had been closed for twelve years. Boarded-up homes, empty shops, and even a deserted schoolhouse testified to its lack of vigor.

Little did I know that this shabby little town would come to define my sense of place. Although I tried several times to leave, seeking career opportunities and even true love, forty years later I'm still here.

Mary Yelenick understood why. She and husband Frank, both natives, owned the town's only liquor store during the tough times. Bidding me goodbye before one of my futile attempts to carve a life elsewhere, she patted me on the arm. "You come back, dear. You're one of us now," knowing I would have to leave before discovering I was already home.

CHAPTER ONE

Crested Butte, 1964…
I Am Smitten

Crested Butte schoolhouses, 1969

IT SNOWED the morning following our June 5, 1964, arrival.

The day after, I roamed muddy streets, lonely and homesick, hating this place I'd been dragged to.

Years later, listening to people raving about falling in love with the town the moment they drove down the hill, I reflect on my first summer here—occasionally aloud. "It was small and dirty. No culture, no kids my age, no shops, and you had to drive thirty miles to Gunnison to wash clothes. Whenever I wore sandals, the coal dust in the street turned my feet black to the ankles."

Unlike many who now are attracted by the beauty, skiing, or friends, my siblings and I came with our parents. My stepfather had enrolled in a summer-long seminar for doctors and lawyers at Dr. Hubert Winston Smith's Law Science Academy.

We rented the Bishop House, one of the homes that Dr. Smith bought in the 1950s and '60s for a pittance when their owners left town, seeking work after the mines closed. In 1964 he charged his academy participants $100 per week for the tiny houses—an outrageous sum at the time, according to my stepfather.

The Bishop House is on Third Street across from the Company Store. Then as now, it was long and skinny, with wild hop-vines curling up its rough wooden siding. Supported by a typical 1880s foundation of loose rocks, the kitchen floor was off kilter enough to tilt the stove, so cooking oil pooled in the back of the frying pan. That didn't faze my mom.

"When I fry the trout, it's like camping," she said.

The front was a mudroom where my two-year-old brother, Kurt, slept in his crib. When the family dined at Lil and Phil Hyslop's Grubstake Bar and Grill, we took turns walking around the corner to peek into the window to make sure he was okay.

Beyond the mudroom were the living room, kitchen, shed, and coal shed, in that order, all connected one behind the other. My sisters and I shared a second-floor loft. We liked to peer out the window at midnight on Saturdays to watch the college kids stagger from the Mineshaft, a 3.2 beer joint in the basement of the Company Store. I couldn't set foot in a 3.2 bar; you had to be eighteen to buy the reduced-alcohol-content beer. At twenty-one you could hit the hard liquor.

But there were special moments. Our first week we found a loaf of homemade bread on our table. "Oh, that's from Grandma Stimac," we were told. "She always bakes bread to welcome a new neighbor." And as the summer progressed and the hillsides turned a lush green, I marveled at the sparkling streams (which I later learned were irrigation ditches) meandering through hay meadows. The mountains, still glazed with snow, encircled the town, set like a diamond whose facets of tin roofs reflected the sun.

After a few weeks I met a girl my own age, Henrietta Raines, who wrote a small social news column for the *Crested Butte Chronicle*. She introduced me to Nettie Kapushion, a

The Bishop House in 1995, our first home in Crested Butte, looks just as it did in 1964.

rancher's daughter, whom I sometimes saw sitting in the back row of the Princess Theater with her boyfriend, Paul Panian Jr. Henrietta had her eye on Dr. Smith's son, Steve. The other four available boys fit into one car "cruising main street" for girls—sleeves cut out of their tight tee-shirts to show off their muscles, a la James Dean.

Toward the end of summer, after a stint helping Henrietta ferret out gossip for her column, I was successful in lobbying my parents for a bus ticket home to Tucson. But returning to the heat of Arizona I realized Crested Butte had already started to grow on me. In fact, the whole family was smitten, and from then on it was winters in Arizona and summers and ski vacations in Crested Butte.

We came back for Christmas and learned to ski when the fledgling ski area on Crested Butte Mountain, two miles north of town (it would be years and a Chapter 11 bankruptcy before it became a "resort"), received a record 100 inches of snow in ten days. Often falling off the J-bar and T-bar lifts, I slogged helplessly in deep powder, frustrated by one of the few sports that didn't come easily for me, and blushing deeply when a handsome but nonchalant ski patrolman offered casual assistance.

The summer of 1965 my family rented a house next door to Henrietta's home on Sopris Avenue. Her younger sister, Gavin, played with mine while Henrietta and I became friends. We camped at Nicholson Lake and stole strawberries at night from the garden up the street. I had crushes on ski patrolmen and ski instructors. Henrietta dated Dr. Smith's son, whom she married the following year.

View toward Gothic Mountain from the ski slopes.

By the summer of 1966 my parents had purchased a house on Elk Avenue and started a business at the ski area. My mother hired a winter manager for her Village Store, and the whole family headed back to Tucson each fall when school started. Vacations from the University of Arizona my freshman and sophomore years were spent skiing Crested Butte. I no longer fell off the T-bar, but returned to Tucson twice with a broken leg.

Undeterred from skiing, I begged my parents to let me attend Western State College in Gunnison, only thirty miles from Crested Butte, but it was known as a party school—rightly so—and they wanted more for me. So for my junior year, I transferred instead to the next best thing, the University of Colorado in Boulder. A five-hour drive from Crested Butte, it was close enough to enjoy holiday skiing.

The summer before the big move to Boulder, I walked up to Nettie Kapushion's house on the edge of town. Knowing her only well enough to say "hi," I gathered my courage and knocked on the door.

"I heard you're going to CU this fall. So am I. Would you like to room together?" I blurted out.

"Um … sure, I guess."

Nettie Kapushion with her aunt Mary Sayre at Tony Mihelich's birthday party in 1993.

Later I learned how difficult it is for Nettie to say no to any reasonable request for fear of hurting someone's feelings. But at that moment all I felt was great relief at her answer. That September we loaded our stuff into my Volkswagon bug and off we went. She proved to be a wonderful roommate, as well as teaching me about this uncomplicated and innocent town of the 1960s. Her mom, Ruth, showered me with compliments and stuffed me with food. Her aunt Adele McCandless, who lived with her husband Ralph on the second floor of the old railroad depot, introduced me to the melt-in-your-mouth Croatian/Slovenian pastry called povitica, also referred to as strudel or potiza.

With the exception of a few ski area employees, almost everyone in Crested Butte had been born and raised here. The men grew up laboring in the coal mines—all of which closed down by the 1950s—or on family ranches, like Nettie's dad, Tony. The women raised the children and kept the house. Money was scarce after the mining companies pulled out and the railroad service was discontinued. Everyone from child to elder worked hard.

Ina McCandless,
Ruth Kapushion's mother
at the wedding in 1976
of her granddaughter
and namesake,
Ina Kristina Kapushion.

*Ruth Kapushion,
in 1986,
was always shy
about being
photographed.*

Most of their parents or grandparents had come from Slavic countries, escaping the poverty and hopelessness of war-torn Europe. Many spoke with native accents. Grandma Stimac, our shy bread-making neighbor, still wore the dark dress, black stockings, and kerchief of the old country.

Honesty was rampant—doors were never locked. Keys were left in ignitions (I often left my camera in the front seat of my car), and you only had to dial four numbers to make a local phone call. There were maybe 100 cars in the whole town. It was rare to meet another one at an intersection. The streets were dirt, and we prided ourselves on having no stoplights. A red caution light hung over the present four-way-stop, where a tattered string of sun-faded Christmas tree lights marked the entrance to town.

My parents' small, white stuccoed Elk Avenue house had a leaky roof, a barn, and a storage shed in the back. Our neighbors were Martha (who became my mother's closest friend) and Whitey Sporcich and their six children, who we had a heck of a time at first keeping straight. In order of age, they are Peggy, Gary, Cathy, Debbie, Helen, and Patty.

Martha and Whitey Sporcich share a laugh in 1975 at his brother Pitsker's annual fish fry near Nicholson Lake. Whitey and Pitsker caught and froze fish all summer preparing for the party.

The Sporciches had one of the greenest lawns in town, which Whitey mowed weekly. As he did, he took a pass with the mower across our yard—a not so subtle hint that we should get out and cut our own grass. Martha worked at the "Hardware," as she called it—which included the only gas pumps in town—owned by her stepfather, Tony Mihelich.

The Sporcich kids did whatever they could to make money, from babysitting to cleaning houses to waiting tables at Frank and Gal's Restaurant and Bar, renowned for Gal's home-made ravioli. It was so homemade you had to order it a day in advance because she made it from scratch, mixing the pasta dough and cutting it into squares, and finally adding the filling. Her recipe was probably passed down through generations of her Italian ancestors, and she was assisted, no doubt, by one or more of the industrious Sporcich girls.

Crested Butte social life centered on its bars. We learned to dance the polka at Frank and Gal's, bounding across the oiled wooden floor in a three-beat, double-time waltz, while Botsie Spritzer or the Mraule brothers played their accordions. Our partners were young and old. Age didn't matter; some of the oldest were the lightest on their feet. All the dancers belted out in unison the refrains to the songs, like "Roll Out the Barrel."

The bars weren't so much a place to drink as a venue in which to catch up on the gossip, dance, and visit with friends. Courtesy dictated buying at least one round of drinks for those sitting with you, but it was considered very bad form to get drunk. Crested Butte natives knew how to nurse a beer for hours. It was a skill I, too, soon learned out of self-preservation, when on occasion I found myself facing five glasses of wine lined up in front of me.

Nettie's dad, Tony Kapushion, owned Tony's Tavern on Elk Avenue. Like the Mineshaft, it was a 3.2 beer joint. Nettie helped wash beer glasses and wiped tables.

Most businesses had a bench outside the front door for socializing or just to sit and watch the world go by. In Crested Butte in the 1960s, there wasn't much world to watch. The post office was (and still is) the ultimate spot for seeing friends and neighbors. I proudly told the catalog folks that no, I don't have a street address, only a box number. Each brass box had a twirling combination lock and a tiny window so you could see if you had mail.

That first summer, silvery-haired postmistress Berneice Gardiner, who knew everyone in town, once scrutinized me over her wire-rimmed glasses from behind the counter, then pulled forth a letter. "I think this is for you." It was addressed to "Freckles," Crested Butte, CO 81224 with an Arizona postmark.

I spent my summers in Crested Butte getting to know its special people, dancing, exploring the backcountry with my family in our old Land Rover, and fishing for trout by the cemetery bridge. We picked wild raspberries growing on the switchbacks on Gunsight Pass, and the Sporciches took us to a secret place to hunt chanterelle mushrooms.

After graduation from CU in 1968, I piled all my belongings back in the VW—by then I'd collected so much there was no room for Nettie, and drove straight home—to Crested Butte, not Arizona. Its intangible mystique had captivated me.

Gal Starika working in her restaurant kitchen in 1969.

Tony Kapushion, Nettie's dad, takes a break from ranching and bartending in 1968.

There was a simple explanation why, although it took me a while to figure it out. People refer to "a sense of community" in trying to pin down its appeal. Here's the secret: the town was one huge family, literally. Nettie helped me understand who was related to whom and who wasn't speaking to whom—it even confused her once in a while, and then she'd stop in mid-sentence. "Oh, I had forgotten I was related to so and so by marriage."

Now that I was a full-time resident, no longer a "summer person," the first order of business after graduation was a job. I approached George Sibley, the new editor of the *Crested Butte Chronicle.*

"Any chance you need a photographer or a reporter?"

"It's pretty much a one-man, four-page operation," he replied. "And I can't pay a salary, but why don't you go take a shot of Frank Starika for an interview I'm writing. If it turns out, I'll put your credit line on it."

Though I'd been a writer throughout high school and college, and editor of my high school paper, my photographic experience had been limited to the usual childhood snapshots with my trusty Brownie Hawkeye. I'd learned the nuts and bolts of printing during a photographic course my senior year at CU. Setting up a makeshift darkroom in the storage area of my mother's store, I stacked liquor cartons for countertops and carried water from the bathrooms next door.

Armed with my graduation gift, a Pentax camera, I walked over to Frank and Gal's house on Sopris Avenue, catching Frank during a rare moment when he wasn't behind their bar on Elk Avenue. Because I didn't have enough money yet to buy a flash, I took the picture outside.

When I showed George Sibley the photo, he was impressed. "Hey, you got him with a new cigar. I've never seen him with a long cigar. He usually just chews on that stub in the bar."

That resulted in my second assignment—Emil Lunk, who played his bandonium at town celebrations and fish frys. Sans flash, I photographed him in his living room, illuminated by window light, holding his instrument that looks like a squeezebox and sounds like an accordion. His deeply lined face, with only a hint of a smile, is framed by the red silk bandana he wore as part of his costume. Again George was pleased. He didn't realize it at the time, but he had launched my photographic career.

After shooting about twelve such portraits of different Crested Butte "old-timers," I matted the prints, and the subjects graciously indicated their approval by signing the mats in a graceful cursive that you rarely see today.

The lives of these men, most of whom really weren't that old chronologically—perhaps only fifty-five to sixty-five—bridge the time between the closing of the last coal mine in 1952 and the opening of the ski area in 1961. From the perspective of us newcomers, they were old-timers. They had stuck out the tough times. The title was one of respect, and I think they were proud of it.

Frank Starika invited me to hang the photographs on the walls of his bar. Before long all the old guys who came in for a beer were buying me drinks and wanting their picture in

My first assignment:
Frank Starika in the
summer of 1968
at his home on
Sopris Avenue.

Emil Lunk, at home in 1968, played his bandonium at town celebrations.

what they fondly referred to as the "Rogue's Gallery," even though they never came right out and said so. Frank allowed me to wander behind the bar in the afternoons, usually a "no no" unless you were a bartender, so I could shoot from a better angle. The men protested weakly, "Look out, Sandy, you'll break the camera."

Shy though I was, I ignored them. It became a challenge to capture them relaxed and un-posed. I shot only a few frames—quickly—before returning to my drink.

Soon I was photographing the women; my original twelve portraits ballooned to a col-lection of about eighty. Martha Sporcich often hid her face from my lens. "I'm not old enough to be an old-timer," she told me with a scowl.

While I was slowly becoming accepted during the late 1960s and early '70s, the first hippies and dropouts of my generation started trickling into Crested Butte. The old-timers were tolerant at first. Later they complained about their being "trust-funders," subsisting on monthly checks sent from Mom and Dad, and doing drugs. They felt the newcomers didn't share their industrious work ethic. Unshaven, uncut, unwashed, and often partially un-dressed—that's how the locals saw them.

The hippies saw nirvana: "I'm free, my dog is free." There was so little traffic that dogs could lie undisturbed in the middle of a street for hours. The cost of living was cheaper then. All any "trust-funder" really needed to "drop out" was a part-time job and a bedroom.

To the extreme displeasure of my mother, I took to wearing tattered jeans and skimpy halter-tops, but I still resided at home. Other people dropped so far out, they were living up in the woods. Dave Coney, who bought a small mining claim near the top of Washington Gulch, fixed up the cabin and outhouse to host all his friends at wild parties—winter or summer—and to ski what they eventually named Coney's Ridge.

Coney's nearest neighbors were Bill and Mary Frame, who after founding the Alpineer Sports Shop purchased the mining ghost town of Elkton and renovated a couple of cabins, where they lived year-round. Their only mode of winter transportation was cross-country skis, supplemented by an old snowcat they purchased from the ski area after Mary had their first baby. They hauled water from the creek, cooked on a wood stove, carried all their sup-plies from town on their backs during the winter, and dug a new hole for the outhouse every spring.

The political atmosphere slowly changed as the town grew. Long-time residents were displaced on the town council by the new arrivals—the loss of control alienating many of them. Loose dogs were a continual problem.

A new middle class also began to settle here with the purchase of the ski area by the Callaway family of Georgia in 1970. The houses Dr. Smith got for a song were repurchased for a fortune and rehabilitated by trust-fund hippies, and by Oklahomans and Texans want-ing to escape the summer heat. Bright-eyed arrivals convinced themselves they could make a killing on their shop or restaurant. In their optimism, they overlooked the five months of spring and fall with no income from skiers or fishermen, and soon went broke and left.

Not everyone was just passing through. Jerry and Tena Sampson bought the Grubstake from Lil and Phil Hyslop in the late '60s and offered family-style dinners for ski patrolmen

Frank Hodgson in 1969 became part of the "Rogue's Gallery."
Frank had worked the Baxter Lode up Washington Gulch seeking gold.

Tony Gallowich, an ex-miner, was employed by the ski area.
In 1969 he was the bottom lift operator on the T-bar where I shot this photo.

Ann Panian, Paul Panian's wife, in 1975, with the old railroad water tower in the background.
Their son Paul Jr. was Nettie Kapushion's first boyfriend.

Paul Panian in 1969. He shared T-bar lift operator duties with Tony Gallowich.

living on beggars' wages. Western State College graduates spent winters ski instructing and waiting tables, and summers doing construction work. Many started small businesses and stayed to raise families. Tenacious and clever entrepreneurs like Allen Cox, who purchased the Nordic Inn in 1970, and Eric Roemer and Lyn Heutschy, who remodeled an old house on Elk Avenue into the popular Penelope's Restaurant in the early '70s, persevered and succeeded. Others, like myself, spent years in the "three job shuffle." I photographed and wrote for the newspaper, cocktail waitressed, and assisted at my mother's store. The ski area provided income for the natives as well—many working as lift operators, waitresses, cooks, maids, and the like.

The newcomers brought with them a joie de vivre; a devil-may-care attitude, inventing unique ways to have fun and celebrate the paradise they had found here. They gave us Flauschink, Vinotok, the Mountain Theatre, the softball league, mountain biking, extreme skiing, and telemarking, just to name a few.

It was a golden time, a treasure trove for me both photographically and as a writer—an unending source of feature stories and photo opportunities of all the new events, plus old customs like the July Fourth celebration, the Memorial Day parade, Pitsker's Fish Fry, and Christmas caroling. Many of the old-timers whose photos hung on Frank and Gal's walls agreed to interviews for the publications I worked for over the years—first the *Chronicle,* then the *Crested Butte Pilot,* which I founded in 1972, several Gunnison newspapers, the now-defunct *Mountain Sun,* and the *Crested Butte Magazine.*

Next thing I knew, forty years had passed since my first summer in Crested Butte. My freckles faded to wrinkles, and polka parties now occur three times a year instead of once a week. The town has outgrown two post offices and is overflowing a third. Most of my portrait subjects have passed on. The photos now grace the walls of the Crested Butte Mountain Heritage Museum, renovated from its days as Tony's Conoco. Newcomers of the 1970s have become what are jokingly referred to as "new old-timers." And people kept saying to me, "Why don't you do a book?"

CHAPTER TWO

Tony Mihelich and the Hardware

Tony Mihelich in 1969.

Tony, do you mind if I take your picture?"

He smiled his assent with gentle blue eyes, standing quietly in his denim overalls and ballcap next to the passenger window as he pumped our gas. I quickly snapped about four frames. It was 1969, shortly after I had shot my photo of Frank Starika chomping on a new cigar for an article George Sibley ran in the *Crested Butte Chronicle*.

Although I had gotten to know him somewhat, it wasn't until 1988 that I officially interviewed Tony Mihelich. Over the years I had photographed him many times for the newspapers: on a motorcycle loaned for a fun shot by a rider gassing up; holding up packets of seeds from the spring planting rack in the Conoco; shoveling snow off his roof; and with Colorado governor Roy Romer under the world-record elk rack that hung over the back counter. My first photo was the best, though, and because I shot so fast, I think it accurately reflected his honest, unassuming self before he had a chance to be self-conscious.

The eight-point rack was from a bull elk taken by John Plutt of Crested Butte in 1899. He shot the big guy in the Dark Canyon of Anthracite Creek, twelve miles west of town, and gave the antlers to John Rozich, who passed them to his stepson Ed Rozman. Ed and Tony Rozman did the footwork to have them certified as a world record on March 19, 1961. The antlers were mounted to a head and neck, and then displayed at the National Western Stock Show. By the time our family arrived, it was on the wall near the back of the Hardware and attracted tourists looking for more than a tank of gas.

"Is that *the* elk?" they'd query, pocket camera cocked.

"Yes," replied Tony.

"Are you John Plutt?"

"No."

And Tony continued with his work—finding hummingbird feeders or garden hoses for his customers.

Owner/operator of the Crested Butte Hardware and Auto Supply Company, also known as Tony's Conoco or the Hardware, for more than half a century, Tony became a tourist attraction in his own right. To both locals and the summer homeowners, he and his Hardware were a constant. He opened the Conoco daily at eight a.m. and worked until nine-thirty or ten in the evening, taking a short break for dinner at around five. Sunday he closed for early-morning Mass, then reopened for the rest of the day. You could always find fishing gear and licenses, tires, tools, gloves, gardening implements, kitchen utensils, and automotive gadgets—you name it, he usually had it in those curved glass cabinets or hanging from the walls. Sometimes, though, he'd shake his head at the request, and most locals knew the phrase by heart: "It's on order. It'll be in on Friday."

The Hardware was the oldest continually run business in town. John McCosker built the structure at the corner of Fourth Street and Elk Avenue as a blacksmith and hardware store in 1883, installing the first gas pump in 1911—a hand-cranked version. Bill Whalen purchased the property in 1922, naming it the Crested Butte Hardware and Auto Supply Company. A Gunnison County commissioner and one-time mayor of Crested Butte, Bill was grandfather to our neighbor Martha Sporcich. Bill's two sons-in-law, Roger Nelson and John Campbell (Martha's father and uncle), ran the business.

After Martha lost her father in 1935 at age eight, her mother, Helen Nelson, was left to raise four children. Four years later, Tony Mihelich, who had hired on at the Hardware at the age of thirty-six, married Helen. The following year he bought out John Campbell's share of the business. Tony and Helen never had children, but he treated his stepchildren as his own.

Marie Campbell in 1974. Martha Sporcich's aunt, Marie lived across Fourth Street from the Conoco. She once showed us trunks full of her handmade quilts. Deprecating her efforts, she'd say, "Now what am I going to do with all these?"

The Croatian Hall, left, in 1974, was Tony's birthplace when it was located on Elk Avenue.
In the 1960s it served as the lecture hall for Dr. Hubert Winston Smith's Law Science Academy.

A humble, kind man, Tony was modest about his life but did reveal a few details during our interview. He was born in the back apartment of the St. Mary's Lodge of the Croatian Fraternal Union, then on Elk Avenue, on November 25, 1903, to John and Mary, who emigrated from Croatia. John worked in the mine and later became a bartender at the Croatian Hall's saloon before it was moved to its present location on Second Street.

Tony told me, "My first job after finishing the eighth grade was working in Mike Fisher's grocery store for fifty cents a day. Then I hauled freight, mail, and provisions from the train depot to mining camps, and later delivered coal to houses all over town."

A couple of summers, he dug potatoes at the Lucero Ranch at Jack's Cabin, now known as the Roaring Judy Ranch. During Prohibition he rented the Croatian Hall and ran the saloon, serving soft drinks and homemade apple cider. He could play pool with the best of them and was an excellent baseball player as well; his favorite positions were shortstop and pitcher. (I learned years later that he had been offered a contract with a major league baseball team.) He also served a six-year stint as town treasurer before ending up at the Hardware.

The Hardware had been a Conoco dealership since 1925 and was the first gas station in town. "The Conoco Company told me that I'm the oldest continual dealership in the country," Tony said. It was big news in 1983 when Conoco made Tony take down the old faded neon sign and put up a new wooden one. "The sign is historical," protested the locals. So Conoco promised to send a refurbished neon sign. Sometime later the old rounded-top gas

     TONY MIHELICH AND THE HARDWARE

pumps were replaced with angular, modern ones. But for the most part things were pretty quiet from the 1950s through the 1980s. Tony and his stepdaughter Martha just pumped gas and sold supplies.

I asked Martha, "When did you start working in the Conoco?" Although she was unsure of the exact date, Martha remembers her first day.

"I think it was in the '60s—I had all my six kids by then, and I looked down the street from our house and saw he was real busy, running around and such. I called him up and he said, 'If you could just come up and give me a hand . . .'"

Martha gave him a hand almost daily since then and became his partner and right-hand woman. She never called it the Conoco. To her it was always "the Hardware." Tony and Martha together managed the business—pumped gas, kept the books on the old rolltop

The Slogar Bar, across the street from the Croatian Hall, in 1976 before its renovation.
It was one of several drinking establishments lining Second Street, the route most miners took home.

desk on the east wall next to the window, waited on customers, washed the glass cabinets, locked the money in the two old safes next to the desk every night, and oiled the wooden floor.

When their mother died in 1973, Martha and her sister June Rozman [wife of Ed] took turns having Tony to dinner. I used to see Tony from our Elk Avenue window. He'd lock the front door of the Hardware at five p.m. and walk to the Sporcichs', next door to us, for dinner. Or he'd walk up Elk Avenue to Second Street to the Rozmans'. After the Rozmans left town and Tony got older, Martha drove up Elk Avenue late every afternoon to bring him home for dinner and then take him back to the Conoco.

Although she occasionally groused about the work to my mother privately, years later she admitted, "I idolized Tony. I could do anything I wanted. He never got mad. And he really liked my kids." Martha and Whitey's son, Gary, moved in with Tony for a few years, taking care of his big white house and its lawn on Second Street across the alley from Rozman's.

At the time of our interview, Tony at age eighty-five was still working full-time, never complaining, and rarely slowing down. He shoveled snow from the roof and from in front of the pumps, and polished the ornate, coal-fired, shiny silver potbelly stove, the only source of heat in the building for at least eighty-five years. In the winter, a regular crew of old-timers gathered around its warmth, chewing the fat and trading stories.

"Remember those girly magazines Tom Snellar hid under the cushion of his chair by the potbelly?" Martha chuckled. "We laughed quite a bit at that," she recalled.

And who could forget when the stove had been featured in a Levi's jeans advertisement, with Tommy Snellar surrounded by pretty young models in Levi's?

Tony outlived many of the men who used to sit by the potbelly, or on the bench outside.

"Ever take much time off?" I asked Tony, knowing the answer but wanting to hear it just the same.

"No, not really. But I used to do a lot of fishing. I think as long as I'm healthy, I'll be working here."

To what did he attribute his longevity and good health, I asked.

"Hard work and living in a good country and clean air."

On his ninetieth birthday in 1993, Tony was honored with a party at the Hardware, planned by his Sporcich grandchildren, who provided an hors d'oeuvres spread over the back counters. The whole town turned out to wish him many more years of good health. He wore a big smile and a corsage on a sweater over a simple shirt tucked into dark trousers. Later, assisted by a couple of great-grandchildren, he blew out the two candles on a cake. Then he unfurled a gift from the town preschool—a banner that read "Happy Birthday, Tony," signed by each child.

The Hardware was closed for business that night. All the customers were already inside. Every native in the county and most of Tony's relatives were there, including his sister Margaret and her husband, Rudy Malensek, of Gunnison, and June and Ed Rozman, and of course all the Sporciches. There were June and John Krizmanich and their son; Nettie Kapushion's family, including even her aunt Mary Sayre from Denver; John and Frances

June Rozman,
Martha Sporcich's sister,
in 1982.

Tommy Snellar in his favorite chair by the Conoco potbelly in 1980. A common sight in his old truck, Tommy kept his dog, Blackie, by his side.

Somrak, Betty Spehar, Darlene Cobai, and Michele and Myrtle Veltri; the mayor and town council, who presented him with a framed certificate; and many, many others from out of town as well. You could hardly walk from one end of the Hardware to the other for the crowd of people. All we needed was a polka band to complete the party.

A couple of years later, Tony started to slow down. Martha's children had long since flown the nest but always pitched in when needed, and she divided her time between her home, the Hardware, and caring for Tony as his health failed. "I made him a milkshake and took it up to him at his house every day. My girls took turns looking in on him," she said.

Tony died at home on Christmas Day, 1996, at age ninety-three, attended by his granddaughter Cathy.

Martha closed the Hardware and after the estate was settled put the building up for sale. Roger Rozman, Ed's son, took the elk rack down; it currently hangs in the Chamber of Commerce office at the four-way stop. The window display remained for years. Folks peering in the padlocked door saw the glass cabinets, snow shovels and tires hanging on the walls, and the cold potbelly. A son-in-law of Martha's inherited the rolltop desk and took it to California. One of the safes went to another branch of the family; the other sat empty next to where the desk had been.

After two years of fundraising and negotiations, the Crested Butte Mountain Heritage Museum purchased the building in September 2001 with donations from many of Tony's former customers. A major grant from the Colorado State Historic Fund stipulated that the renovation of the building adhere to National Register of Historic Places guidelines, as befitting a 100-plus-year-old building. The goal was to keep it intact while bringing it up to code and readying it for use as a museum. The slightly bowed interior plasterboard walls were not replaced with drywall and so do not take well to nails. It made hanging my oldtimer photo collection quite a challenge. The photos are slightly askew, which may reflect the subjects themselves—informal, hardworking, and fun loving. Tony's 1969 portrait, which he signed "A. J. Mihelich," overlooks his desk by the east window.

When the museum finally reopened in the renovated Conoco in the summer of 2003, we were all relieved to see that much looked as it had when Tony and Martha locked the door for the last time ten years earlier. The side shed was made into the museum store. The garage where Tony stored cars had become display space, with an office overhead. The glass cabinets and display cases remained, filled with Tony's leftover stock. The oiled wooden floor still supported the old safe, to which Martha has forgotten the combination. The rolltop desk came back from California, and next to the potbelly stove sits Tom Snellar's old chair.

Tony would've approved.

CHAPTER 3

Rip-Sawing Through
the Fourth of July

Wheeling to win. Cowboys competing in the wheelbarrow race in 1968.

Kaboom!

Another Independence Day in Crested Butte had been jump-started by an early-rising ex-miner who lit a stick of dynamite on a nearby hillside. I heard it dimly through sleep and felt the vibrations rattling the windows. In the late 1960s this traditional six a.m. explosion was supposed to get everyone out of bed and raring to celebrate, but those who started partying the previous night probably buried their aching heads, groaning into their pillows. For surely they, and probably I, weren't going to make it to the first event of the day: the Gothic to Crested Butte Run, Walk, Crawl 1/3rd Marathon.

The race was mostly George Sibley's inspiration, who thought Gothic, home to the Rocky Mountain Biological Laboratory (RMBL) since 1929, and populated in the summer by world-class scientists and researchers, seemed much farther from Crested Butte's hippies and ex-miners than eight miles by car.

"The marathon was a way of bringing everyone closer together," recalled the then *Crested Butte Chronicle* editor, who worked out the details and shared the organizing with Chris Johnson, the son of RMBL's founder. The race was for fun, just perambulating oneself from Gothic to Crested Butte by running, walking, or crawling—if that's what it took.

Runners set off from Gothic at eight a.m. and completed the 8.2 miles (give or take a few feet) in front of the Old Rock Schoolhouse, where they crossed a line of flour poured onto the dirt street. A couple of people sat with stopwatches or wristwatches and a clipboard, recording the results. The first racers across the line were often students from the lab—fit twenty-year-olds—and Western State College track team members. George and his three-year-old son Sam held the record for the longest time—four hours. George recalls many precious minutes wonderfully wasted (or perhaps not) admiring flowers or birds. Abby Endner was the oldest racer/walker, and, at age eighty-something, fell and broke her wrist. Not realizing the extent of her injury, she cheerfully continued, waving it to the photographer.

By the time most of the runners ran, walked, or crawled into town, and the rest of us rolled out of bed, it was time for the ten a.m. parade, leaving from the Old Town Hall at Second Street. Crested Butte prided itself for being the only place where parades go down the main drag and then turn about and come back up. When I first came to town it made a lot of sense. The parade wasn't more than half a block long, and that way the spectators got to see both sides of the floats. As the parade lengthened year after year until it stretched from Second Street to Fifth Street, turning it all around for the trip back up became a logistical nightmare. The RMBL folks, with scientific ingenuity, simply marched up the street backwards. Their majorette led the ragtag band of students, clothed only in the large leaves of the false hellebore (skunk cabbage), that grows in profusion around Gothic, blowing kazoos and whistles, and waving butterfly nets. Hummingbird researcher David Inouye walked the whole parade route on stilts.

George Sibley in 1978. An incomparable wit, he could outpun anyone in town.

By 2003, the parade was starting at First Street and stretching out the road to the ski area. Reversal for the return journey took so long that many spectators starting leaving. So in 2004, breaking the tradition, it began at Seventh Street and proceeded up Elk Avenue to Second Street. One way only.

Early on, you didn't have to sign up to be in the parade. You could just show up, which, if you started your celebration the previous night, had varying results. Either you gave up your stupendous idea for a float concocted a few hours earlier after several beers and went back to bed to sleep it off, or you dragged yourself out to help some friends throw it together. "Floats" were often pick-up trucks with hand-lettered signs duct-taped to the doors, accompanied by wildly costumed locals.

George Sibley and his bride-to-be, Barbara Kotz, came up with a first-prize winner in 1968. Her woodcarving studio, the Alphabet, was in the small red building on Elk Avenue that once served as the ski area office. On shelves around the walls, she nailed each letter of the alphabet carved in different fonts. People saw her letters and the name of the business and somehow made a vague connection to newspapers. It should have been obvious from the sawdust-strewn floor that, as Barbara patiently explained, "This is not the newspaper office. It is across the street." She directed them to Tony's Tavern, where George used a former liquor storage closet in the back as an office.

So for the parade George constructed a small one-hole outhouse, complete with toilet paper on a holder, that was hauled on a trailer hitched to the back of Barbara's Volkswagen bug. On the front of the car a sign read, "Contrary to Popular Opinion the Alphabet is not a Newspaper, it's a Sign Shop." George's sports editor, old-timer Botsie Spritzer, who wrote a weekly fishing column (or rather dictated it to George, who typed it) sat on the "throne" reading the *Chronicle*. Above the door was a white hand-lettered sign: "Reading Room." George, portraying an old-time newspaper editor, was clad in an 1880s-type costume complete with a flowered vest made by local seamstress Adele Bachman, and a long black coat, string tie, and hat once worn by Botsie's dad. Tall and thin, he looked rather Abe Lincol-nesque, positioned next to the outhouse and waving to the crowd, a broad grin across his prominent jaw.

A sign over the throne read, "Recommended by Dunkin' Hinds." Others read, "Do not flush while train is in station. Please remain seated during entire performance," and "Nearly every house in Crested Butte has a *Chronicle* . . . someplace."

As George tells it, "The trailer we used for the outhouse was hanging around in Botsie's friend's yard at Second Street and Elk Avenue, and Botsie swore it was fine with his friend if we used it. It was a genuine old wooden wagon with wooden wheels under iron rims. The wood had shrunk over the years, so we wired the rims on. It was a precarious operation. We kept having to stop and rewire the rims during the parade."

That memorable parade included a small marching band, complete with a bass drum. The Grubstake Bar and Grill sported a sign on its truck: "We'll stake our reputation on our steaks." My mom and stepfather hooked together our two old Land Rovers rear to rear. My brother, Kurt, and older sister, Laura, sat atop in gigantico Mexican straw sombreros that

ABOVE: *Volunteer firefighters competing in the hose cart races up and down Elk Avenue in 1973.*

OPPOSITE: *My brother, Kurt Taylor, thought the outhouse was for real.*

my mom sold in her Village Store. Mayor Lyle McNeill rode on the hood of an old Forest Service Jeep waving the American flag. And there were the usual riders on horseback. Snow fence borrowed from the ski area kept the crowds from spilling onto Elk Avenue; the visitors outnumbered the locals. Everyone partied in Crested Butte all day and traveled to Gunnison for the fireworks at night.

The street events on Elk Avenue after the parade have varied throughout the years. In the 1960s and 1970s, Johnny Cobai parked the county's lowboy, a trailer used to haul heavy equipment, at the Third Street intersection. Some of the contests took place atop this makeshift elevated stage to allow the crowd a better view of the action, including the pie eating, ladies' nail-driving, and my favorite, the ladies' ripsaw contest.

An old-timer donated the use of his ripsaw—a four-foot-long bladed, toothed saw with a wooden handle at each end. Two-women teams took a crack at a section of log, up to two feet in diameter, supported by a sawhorse and held down by a couple of burly guys hunkered on each end. Fastest sawyers won.

The trick wasn't necessarily in the muscle, although that was a big part of it. It was the teamwork, the finesse and rhythm. Most of all it was about letting your partner pull as you refrained from pushing. A secret known to every old-timer who felled large trees with this

CHRONICLE
Here's the Place, folk.
Subscribe to the Chronicle!
READING ROOM
Do not flush while train is in station
PLEASE REMAIN SEATED DURING ENTIRE PERFORMANCE
BASEMENT FOR

Adele Bachman, Crested Butte town clerk, served as a marshal on Fourth of July 1972, but took time out to win the ripsaw contest.

saw, it was whispered to the contestants by their boyfriends. "Never push. Let her pull the saw toward her, then you pull it toward you." If in the heat of action, egged on by the crowd, you forgot this sage wisdom and pushed, the saw buckled and popped up out of the cut. Precious seconds were lost while you tried to maneuver it back in place, your partner twisting it left while you yanked right, and vice versa.

My sister Kathy and I partnered at least once.

"Stop pushing, let me pull," she would shout over the cheers of the crowd.

"I am, I am! Shut up and saw."

When we were on, almost no one could touch us. Only Adele Bachman, who had muscles, finesse, *and* bagged her own deer each year, had us both beat, regardless of whom she partnered with.

Joe Rozman, who ran the sawmill next to his house at the west end of Elk Avenue, provided the log for the sawing and the long iron nails and flat-sided log for the ladies' nail-driving contest. He also dumped a truckload of sawdust into the vacant lot next to Barbara's Alphabet building. Scattering the dimes that the organizing committee gave him into the sawdust, he watched amused as little kids thrashed through the pile, throwing up handfuls of dust. Equally amused, I watched him shyly take a handful of change out of his own pocket and add it to the melee.

Until the mining and milling operations shut down at the Peanut Mine north of town, miners competed in timed hard-rock drilling contests, where they jammed a two-inch-diameter electric drill bit, similar in size and force to a jack hammer, into rocks trucked in for the occasion. For years, the results of their efforts, large boulders with deep, narrow holes in them, sat around the vacant lots on Elk Avenue, looking like odd-shaped pieces of Swiss cheese.

These miners, along with every other able-bodied man, belonged to the volunteer fire department, when a two-wheeled cart with a length of fire hose rolled over the reel was the town's only fire-fighting equipment. The Fire Protection District and pancake breakfasts were not even on the horizon in the 1960s. Competing in the hose-cart races, two-man

Joe Rozman in 1979, tough on the outside, a softie within.

Vonda Rozman, Joe's wife. Memorial Day, 1981.

teams ran their carts to the "fire," pulled out the hoses, and then wound them back on the reels and raced to the fire station—located in the Old Town Hall.

Other events included the tug-of-war originally down Elk Avenue and in later years across Coal Creek at the Totem Pole Park; a ladies' slipper kick, where the contestant placed her shoe on the toe of her foot, took a giant swing back with her leg and let loose; foot races for all ages and sexes, and boys' and girls' shoe scrambles.

All in all, those Fourth of July celebrations of the 1960s were humdingers—right down to the regular late afternoon cloudburst when everyone scattered, seeking shelter, and the time a local cowboy grabbed me in the street and planted a juicy kiss on my unwilling mouth. Thirty years later when he asked me to photograph him for my old-timer series, I hadn't forgotten. "Come and get me if I'm not home by 4:00 sharp," I instructed my husband.

The evening polka party crowned the Fourth of July celebration. My sister and I stomped breathlessly with almost everyone in town at Frank and Gal's or the Grubstake, where Johnny and Tommy Mraule laid into their accordions and we sang "Just Because."

For as long as anyone could remember, the volunteer firemen organized the celebration. But, as George Sibley recalls, "There was no formal July 4th celebration planned for 1970. They felt it was getting too big and was too much work. I remember saying in the council meeting, 'Well, we gotta have a Fourth of July!' So I volunteered, and one shot at it was enough for me."

I obviously didn't learn from George's experience, because the next thing I knew, it was 1974, and Lyle McNeill, who had taken over the organizing, roped me into helping. I can only surmise he decided since I was reporting on the July 4th doin's as editor of the *Crested Butte Pilot,* I may as well help pull it together. Being a newspaper editor in a small town carried with it responsibility other than just gathering the news and printing it. Or as George told me, "There's a thin line between reporting things and making things to report."

Today with the Chamber of Commerce running the Fourth of July celebration, all the newspaper editors do is send their photographers to shoot a few parade and street pictures. By 2004, the street events were relegated to Third Street, and a flatbed truck, provided by a construction company, held an announcer and a rock band. A street dance seemed to be the main focus. The wheelbarrow race was history, but they'd added a female arm-wrestling event and men's log-sawing competition.

The RMBL researchers, as always, don their green wilted skunk cabbage skirts. The kids toss water balloons and run the three-legged race. Serious water fights erupt at the end near Kochevar's—a relatively new development escalating during the 1980s and 1990s when the fire department entertained the crowd by showing off its pumper truck—(a far cry from the hose cart races of the 1960s). Alas, I haven't heard the dynamite in ages.

The small-town Fourth of July flavor is still there, albeit a bit more tourist oriented. But when I look at my photos from 1968, I get a deep urge to call my sister. "Hey, Kathy, let's do the ripsaw this year. I promise not to push."

CHAPTER 4

Rudy Sedmak

Rudy Sedmak in 1980, relaxing in front of Tony's Conoco.

$\mathbf{I}$F YOU REMEMBER when the old Keystone double chairlift was called "Rudy's Lift," you'd *almost* qualify as a Crested Butte old-timer. Born and raised here, Rudy Sedmak is a bona fide old-timer. As one of the first ski area employees, he was the head operator of the lift from 1969, when it was built, until his retirement in 1980. Rudy recalled, "I still run into people in the summer who ask me, 'Remember when you put me on the lift twenty years ago?'"

I remember only too well. It was my first day of work as a snow hostess supervisor in 1978. I boarded the lift with Terri, a fellow hostess, who was about to sit in the chair closest to Rudy. But at the last minute before the lift swept us up and away, Rudy reached across her and handed me a heavy fire extinguisher to juggle with my ski poles.

"Hey, Sandy. Take this up top, would you?"

I grabbed the extinguisher, sort of. As I vainly tried to hold on, it slipped out of my gloved hands and the chair slipped out from under my behind. A split second later Rudy shut off the lift. Terri and I, in our brand new uniforms, were dumped on the snow, an embarrassed bundle of skis, poles, that damn fire extinguisher, and wounded pride. Rudy put us all back together again, carefully handed me the source of our mortification, and sent us on our way. Rudy and I still laugh about it, but he's never told me why he didn't hand it to Terri instead of me.

I first met Rudy in 1964. My stepfather had come to attend the Law Science Academy. We were living in the Bishop House, one of the homes Dr. Hubert Winston Smith, the founder of the Law Science Academy, had purchased from unemployed miners in the late 1950s.

"People were begging him to buy their houses because they had no work and had to leave town," Rudy explained to me years later. "Emil Cobai went to Doc Smith and said, 'give me a thousand dollars and you can have my house and everything in it.'"

The Cobai family was still in town when I arrived, so I guess Dr. Smith didn't need any more houses.

"Dr. Smith, who was from Austin, Texas, hired me for $2.50 an hour. I had an impressive title: Head of Maintenance and Construction," quipped Rudy, tongue firmly in his cheek. His job was to caretake Dr. Smith's thirty-eight houses, set up the tables for lectures in the Croatian Hall (now the Crested Butte Club), and bring in the skeletons used by the doctors for demonstrations.

"Dr. Smith was an odd fella. He'd come to the house to visit and in ten minutes be sound asleep. He'd do the same thing at the doctors' and lawyers' lectures," said Rudy.

I attended a couple of those lectures. The lights were turned off for the slide show, and almost immediately snoring echoed from the back of the room.

Emil Cobai in Frank and Gal's in 1982.

Rudy once came to our house to fix a pipe. As he recalled our first meeting, "I hollered at you and your sister and Henrietta and Gavin Raines to turn off that loud music you were dancing to." I, of course, don't remember that introduction in 1964 as vividly as the disastrous encounter on the ski lift more than ten years later.

If you owned an old house in town, chances are Rudy knew its quirks. One summer Rudy stopped by my back yard during his daily walk around town. "Hey, Rudy," I asked. "Why is my yard developing this big depression?"

"It's near the bathroom, right?"

"Yeah. I stack my wood right here every winter close to the back door." I gestured to the scattering of wood chips near the clothesline. "Maybe the ground is getting swayback from the load."

He laughed at my joke but knew the real answer. "Probably the septic tank. When they put in the sewers in the early 1970s, most people just threw planks and dirt over to cover up the septic tanks."

My friend across the street found this out too late, when a sinkhole developed in her back yard that had to be filled with truckloads of expensive dirt.

Throughout his life, Rudy had been a jack of all trades, doing whatever was needed to make a living and support a family. When he wasn't caring for houses and skeletons in the summer, Rudy picked up other jobs. And he confirmed a longtime legend about old-timers keeping their money in the cellar.

"One day Willard Ruggera, Fritz Yaklich, and I were putting in a water line under Stefanic's Grocery. We found coffee cans full of silver dollars and got scared and left. After the bank went broke in 1929, a lot of people wouldn't keep their money in the bank. Tony Stefanic was robbed once a long time ago, but he didn't know how much was missing because he didn't know how much money he had," he explained.

Of Yugoslavian and Austrian descent, Rudy was born in Crested Butte on August 19, 1912. He, his brothers Lewis and Joe, and sisters Mary and "Babe" lived in the graceful white family home on White Rock Avenue. Their grandfather Joe Gallowich had arrived in town in 1879. He told young Rudy that the town was once full of evergreen trees that were all cut down to build the houses. Even the foundation of the Old Town Hall at Third Street and Elk Avenue was built with evergreen stumps.

Rudy started first grade in the Old Rock Schoolhouse. From third through eighth grades, he attended school in a red brick building that was eventually demolished to make room for the school that opened in 1927 and was remodeled into the town offices in the 1990s. Here Rudy finished high school in 1930, after his freshman year at the Old Rock Schoolhouse. He remembers the red brick school as having steam heat that was also piped over to the Old Rock Schoolhouse. "And it was always clanking."

"The teachers were really strict," said Rudy. "No monkeyshining! As soon as school was out for the summer, the kids brought in the wood and coal for the next winter. Then the rest of the summer was ours. We used to climb over the top of Red Lady Mountain into Paradise Basin. We also climbed Gibson Ridge and Crested Butte Mountain with the Plutt brothers."

Rudy explained that the red color on Red Lady used to be much more vivid. "It's from the waste of the red ore from prospecting up there. After a rain the color of the rock turned bright red. The old-timers would say, 'She's washing her hair again.'"

Sports in Crested Butte were an important part of life, Rudy recalled. "We had a baseball team called the Skippers after a kid that skipped school. When the teacher left the room for five minutes, Louie Skoff was out the door. She'd come back and say, 'Well, he skipped again.' We built a diamond up on the Bench. The superintendent lent us lights so we could play at night. But he told us 'no girls up there.'"

*Rudy's brother, Joe Sedmak, affectionately known as "Cheech," sits with Barbara Kotz
on the bench in front of Frank and Gal's in 1968.*

Rudy told me about starting a neighborhood pick-up basketball team whose members included Joe and John Plutt, Tony Orazem, Louie Skoff, and Tony Mihelich. "We beat the high school team. We also played the girls' team, which included the three Gardiner sisters—Berneice, Hazel, and Margaret. They were tougher on us than any boy's team. Beat us every time. Back then, girls were more equal in sports. Berneice played for blood. She didn't care who you were or what you did."

Rudy and his friends used to ride a special train one and a half hours to Gunnison, and back the same night for basketball games. The rivalry between the towns was renowned. "The train ride only took an hour, but it took another half hour to gather the people together," he explained.

Fishing was also a highlight of their summers.

*Mary Sedmak, Rudy and Joe's mother, attending a show featuring my old-timer photos in 1982.
I added her to the line-up.*

"We walked to the second bridge by Niccoli's Ranch and worked our way up to the cemetery bridge and eventually up to O-be-joyful," said Rudy.

In the winter, he had a leg up on getting the best skis. The miners who operated the sawmill up on Big Mine Hill gave him and his friends slab scraps for their homemade skis. A flat grassy area above Belleview Avenue, Big Mine Hill (now known as the Bench), was where the Big Mine and mill were located, along with mule barns and the mine superintendent's house. The house and barns were moved to town in the early 1980s. The other buildings rotted from disuse or were dismantled for their lumber. During the mining days, there were no houses on Belleview—only the coke ovens, where the coal was heated and partially processsed before being loaded on the train and transported to the steel mills in Pueblo. In old photos you can see the train tracks paralleling the line of beehive-shaped coke ovens.

"There were 176 steps up to the top of the Bench. Since I was the closest because I lived on White Rock Avenue, I got the first wooden slabs. Then we slid down the hill on them."

In 1924 at age twelve, Rudy got his first part-time job as a "flunky" in the drugstore located in the Grubstake building on Elk Avenue. "I remember the name of every one of my bosses. My pay there was ten dollars per month, and I worked on weekends and after school until eight."

He also worked for the mortuary on Elk Avenue, run by Joe Land and Tony Matkovich and located next to the Wooden Nickel. The Plutt brothers worked there as well.

The Sedmak family home on White Rock Avenue,
where Rudy's brother, Joe, lived alone until his death in October 2005.

The Washhouse was one of the few buildings left on Big Mine Hill from the mining operations. In 1982, when I shot this photo, it was gradually collapsing and shortly after was dismantled.

"One day we took John Plutt's picture in the casket and showed it to his mom. She took one look at it and said, 'he's gonna *wish* he were dead!'

"We'd put the stiffs up on the "slumber table" and pump the blood out of 'em by hand and put in the formaldehyde. Now they have machines that do it. I cleaned up . . . I did it all," said Rudy. "But it's not like people died every day. So we loafed a lot, too. Ted Coe, the mortician, was always pulling pranks on us. One day I walked in and heard moaning. Ted had climbed in a casket and then he started moving and I didn't wait to see who it was. I ran for the back door, only it was frozen shut."

Later on he was a delivery boy for the Colorado Supply Company in the Company Store. "I had a team of one horse and one mule and everyone laughed at us. I took orders and delivered them the next day. I kept the horses in the barn (now the Old Town Hall at Second Street and Elk Avenue)."

Social life for young Rudy was hanging out with friends, Saturday night parties, and pranks. "Every Sunday we put on our good clothes and walked down the boardwalk from Fifth and Elk to the railroad depot and back. It was a must. We had gangs," explained Rudy. "But the worst thing we did was steal turnips from Pete Stimac, who had the best garden in the county."

Rudy graduated from high school at age sixteen, one of few Crested Butte boys at that time to do so. Many of his peers started working in the coal mines with their fathers at a

RUDY SEDMAK

much younger age. Following graduation, Rudy began the first of what was to be thirty-two years of underground labor in the mines. He partnered with his dad at Peanut Mine, in the Colorado Fuel and Iron's (CF&I) Big Mine, at Keystone Mine, and at Thompson Creek Mine in Glenwood Springs.

"We made about $4.44 a day at the Peanut. We only mined from September to April because no one needed domestic coal in the summer. In the summer we worked at local ranches. One summer I worked at the Lucero Ranch, across the road from the Danni Ranch, down valley picking potatoes for a dollar a day and meals. Another time I was doing haying, irrigating, and fencing for John Rozman."

"I hated working at the Peanut Mine," said Rudy. "The tunnels were low, and we crawled to push the coal out."

I asked him which of his jobs he enjoyed the most.

"I liked mining the best."

I was astounded by his answer. But he certainly had a logical explanation.

"I was out of the weather. There was no snow to shovel and everyone got along well with everyone else. Big Mine was very safe. We were treated very well by CF&I. Later on the salary was comparatively good and the shaft I worked in was six to eight feet high, so you didn't have to stoop while you worked.

"The boys riding back on the train to Crested Butte from World War II saw railroad cars with stickers pasted to the top chunks of coal: 'CF&I Crested Butte coal.' That was a sight."

In 1952, after demand for coal decreased, the railroad closed down. The Keystone Mine superintendent, Nolan Probst, asked Rudy to walk the twenty-eight miles of tracks to Gunnison, count the ties, and mark them with white chalk. "I started at eight in the morning, and Ralph McCandless, who was working for ASR [American Smelting and Refining Company], picked me up in Gunnison at five that afternoon," said Rudy matter of factly. "I marked the good ties with an X and the bad ones with an O." ASR purchased the ties for ten cents each to use for timber for mine shafts.

When the last of the mines closed in 1952–1954, many Crested Butte men sought work elsewhere, Rudy among them. He, Jimmy Christoff, and Billy Verzuh went to Arizona to work as carpenters. Being from Arizona, I was curious as to how he liked it.

"It was pretty wild down there," said Rudy. He declined to be more specific. I got the feeling he wasn't talking about the state, but the company he was keeping.

"I was sending money home to Emmy [Verzuh, whom he married in 1939.] She was buying logs for the cabin we were building on land we purchased near Gothic. You could have bought all of Gothic then for twenty-five dollars in back taxes."

After working in Aspen at the Jerome Hotel and as a caretaker for the Gates Home of Gates Rubber fame, Rudy returned to his hometown, and with John Perko, spent about two years helping to dismantle the mines. The pair, the county and state road maintenance crews, plus the janitor at the school, and the town manager were about the only men working in town at the time.

"Those were pretty lean times." He shook his head ruefully.

John Rozman Sr. in 1988, taking time out from haying his upper ranch next to the ski area road.

Then, as now, you did what you could to keep food on the table. Which is how he came to work for Dr. Smith at the Law Science Academy in the early 1960s when we first met.

Rudy also served on the Crested Butte town council for sixteen years, as the unpaid building inspector for twelve years, and as deputy marshal for two years under Shammy Somrak. At one time, he recalled, there were only 225 people in town, and no one wanted to take on the responsibility of the marshal's job.

"Willard Ruggera was the town manager, and when there was a problem he would call the council and they'd say, 'use your own judgment.'"

Most men in town were fire department volunteers; Rudy served a thirty-eight-year stint. He was also the owner and projectionist of the Princess Theater for twelve years.

Rudy has a lot of stories about the old days, including the Ku Klux Klan parades of the 1920s.

"There was only one black in the area, Milton Byron, who was in an orchestra that came up from Gunnison, and he was well liked. The KKK called themselves 100 percent American, and they wore white robes and carried flags. They used to march down Elk Avenue. But everyone knew who they were. One time Willie Mosher was walking in his Klan robe in the parade. He was real short. So everyone knew him. And his mom called out, 'look at the little son of a b——.'

"They burned a cross on Chocolate Peak above town. There were twenty or thirty of them, and their headquarters was at the Masonic Hall, which was called the Knights of Phythias then."

Many years later, Rudy and I were involved with a project helping the town of Crested Butte, in conjunction with a private research firm, document the historic buildings. Rudy was a whiz at it—he knew exactly who lived in which house when. His sharp memory made him a valuable resource in recounting the history of Crested Butte. My job was to photograph the buildings from all four sides.

One day in 1998 as I focused in on a small white house on Maroon Avenue, a man who looked to be in his forties got out of a car and approached me. "I own that house," he said.

Billy Verzuh in 1992—the cowboy who snatched a kiss from me on the Fourth of July.

Tony Verzuh watches the July 4th parade in 1980. He and his brother, Billy, owned ranches south of and adjacent to Crested Butte, where Tony lived in a house on the corner of Third Street and Maroon Avenue.

Rudolph "Shammy" Somrak Sr. at the Senior Citizens Center on Memorial Day, 1987. Born in Crested Butte in 1915, and brother of John Somrak, he was married to "Babe" Sedmak, Rudy and Joe Sedmak's sister. Shammy served as the Crested Butte marshal from 1955 to 1969, and passed away in 1997.

"Do you mind if I photograph it?" I asked. It was important not to offend any property owners, I'd even had to buy special liability insurance for the job.

"Do you want to see the inside?" he offered. "This was my family home, although I live in Denver now and just come up once in a while."

I jumped at the chance and followed him into a living room that probably hadn't been occupied since the mines closed, with the old furniture still in place, yellowing linoleum floors, peeling flowery wallpaper, wooden wainscoting, low ceilings, and a musty smell.

He went into the bedroom and returned with a box, which he opened. As he lifted up the white pile of heavy cotton before my astonished eyes, a chill ran through me—a Ku Klux Klan robe. I touched it gently. The material was soft and nubby. The man pointed out the owner's initials, T.A., inscribed on the inside of the collar. It belonged to his relative,

     RUDY SEDMAK

Crested Butte Mountain with a plume of snow blowing off its peak in 1989.

Tom Arnott. About five years later I told Rudy about it. He lifted an eyebrow above his long aquiline nose.

"He showed it to you, huh?" He laughed slightly. I think he was surprised, but wouldn't let on. I know I was.

Most of Rudy's reminiscences were from the more peaceful 1950s and 1960s.

"There was no traffic here then. One day there were only two cars on Elk Avenue. They belonged to John Cobai and Lee Starritt and they had a collision on the bridge." He laughed heartily.

And why did he stay when all his friends and co-workers left town in the 1950s?

"There were always the nicest people here. It was like a big family."

When the ski area was built in 1961–1962, Rudy began a new career as a ski lift operator, running the T-bar. He was capable but strict and didn't hesitate to tongue-lash anyone who tried to cut in line. In those days, the only lift lines were during Christmas, and even they were none too long.

"My assistants were Ande Anderson, who had his lapis lazuli mine on Cement Mountain, and Elmer Eflin" (father of Dick Eflin, one of the ski area's founders). During the ski area's bleak period of Chapter 11 bankruptcy in the late 1960s, Rudy was the maintenance man in "the barn." Back then it was a true log barn at the base of the ski area, left over from its ranching days on the Malensek property. Today "the barn" refers to the lower level of the modern Whetstone building, housing snowcats and snowmobiles. When Whetstone was built, the original Malensek barn was moved to Elk Avenue in Crested Butte, where it serves as a retail shop.

Things were pretty makeshift during the bankruptcy period. "We couldn't charge any materials at local stores, but somehow Dave Oberosler and John Gallowich would get what we needed and Ed Rozman would make it. We took everything apart and put it back together."

Ed helped to keep the snowcats running with what little money was allocated to maintenance, plus some skillful tricks with bailing wire. His expertise stood me in good stead the day I drove up "the hill," as we called the ski area, and arrived at the parking lot, smoke pouring out of my car's engine. Ed came out of the barn, took a look under the hood of my old Toyota Landcruiser, and got out his welding torch to fix a leak in the radiator. Not for money, but for the challenge. Made it good as new, and it lasted until I sold the car fifteen years later.

In 1969 rumor had it that the Aspen Ski Corporation was going to buy the bankrupt Crested Butte Ski Area and dismantle it. Rudy said, "At the time, Emmy and I were building a new house on the east side of town. And I was wondering what am I doing building a home if there's no work?"

By the time he retired at age sixty-eight, Rudy had worked on every one of the early lifts—the T-bar, the J-bar, Keystone, and the gondola. His pay was seven dollars per hour. A friend in the ski area's management privately admitted that they could hire two young kids for his salary.

"I remember people would call me at home for a snow report, claiming they trusted me more than the official ski area report," Rudy said.

It was that kind of visibility that resulted in Rudy's selection as the second Flauschink king in 1970. "My queen was Barbara Sibley, and neither one of us was much of a drinker," he said, referring to the Flauschink party tradition of visiting every bar in town. "Many years ago I drank

Ed Rozman in 1982—a genius with a welding torch.

     RUDY SEDMAK

Crested Butte Ski Area in November 1970, Rudy's era, before condominiums and trophy homes.

with Tim Morgan, and I felt like I was drunk for a week afterward. I've never touched the stuff since."

I am convinced that's why Rudy remembered everything so well. He hadn't addled his brain with booze.

He didn't like all the changes here, but admitted, "The town's cleaner and nicer." And remodeled, he might add. But just in case your old miner's house has a problem you can't figure out, go see Rudy. Chances are he'll know exactly what you should do.

January 11, 2004—Rudolph Joseph Sedmak Jr. died in Gunnison after a short illness at age ninety-one. "Rudy's Lift" has been replaced with the Red Lady Express high-speed quad.

CHAPTER 5

Parenting a Newspaper

The Union Congregational Church was a favorite subject of mine.
This photo from 1978 is similar to the one for which I won an award from the Colorado Press Association.

EWLY WED AND STARRY-EYED IN 1971, I agreed to my husband Bill's inspiration. After all, he already had a successful construction business, so why wouldn't we
be successful with an advertising flyer?

We titled it the *Butte Pilot*. One sheet, two sides. The top of each side was devoted to local entertainment, such as it was—a band playing at the Grubstake Bar or the end-of-the-
year Flauschink celebration schedule. We often ran a small column of blurbs on who was
doing what, or occasionally a news story like the announcement of a new chair lift being
built at the ski area. On the back were small maps of the town and the ski area. The rest was
ads. Published during the winter of 1971–1972 by Tree Enterprises, Inc., Bill's construction business name, it brought us a nice supplemental income, although it certainly did not
constitute exciting journalism. Neither of us had an inkling of how that ad flyer would
eventually thrust us into competing in the newspaper world of Crested Butte.

About that time, the *Crested Butte Chronicle,* which had been the town's official newspaper
for as long as anyone could remember, was sold to Myles Arber of New York City. A long-
winded, non-practicing attorney with a fast but not always accurate mouth, Myles offended
so many people that some of the advertisers started an informal boycott. Apparently uncon-
cerned, he rambled on for inches and inches—nay, pages—in the space vacated by the
advertisers. He must not have needed the revenue since he neglected to send out bills for
months at a time.

A low rumble rolled through town. Every time I delivered our ad sheet I heard it.
"Someone ought to start another newspaper."

That someone turned out to be Bill and me.

"You can do it. You practically have a journalism degree," Bill pointed out. "We could
start a paper."

"Yeah, but who would print it? And can we sell the advertising to support it?" I asked.
"And think of all the time it would take."

"I'll do the bookkeeping, send the bills, and mail out the subscriptions," he promised.
"That'll free you up to write and take pictures."

I was doubtful Crested Butte could support two newspapers. It had been a one-
newspaper town almost since its incorporation in 1880. The *Elk Mountain Pilot,* founded in
Irwin and moved to Crested Butte in 1884, discontinued publication in 1949. Crested
Butte was without its own paper until the *Crested Butte Chronicle* began publication on November 7, 1962, with Helen Mann as its publisher. She sold it to a friend of the ski area's
owner, who hired Alan Hegeman as editor from October 1963 to June 1964. Henrietta
Raines, my first friend in Crested Butte, was listed on the masthead as "editorial assistant."
After Alan departed, the *Chronicle* was edited for several years by public relations staff from
the ski area.

The birthplace of the Butte Pilot, *soon to be the* Crested Butte Pilot,
was my mother's house at 422 Elk Avenue where we lived as newlyweds.

The front page often featured a long social news column. That's what a small town was about, so it made sense. Fresh from high school, where I had been the newspaper editor, I dropped by the little red building on Elk Avenue in 1964 to meet the editor who replaced Alan. He "hired" me for a couple of months to proofread the stories, and I was awarded the title of "chief copyreader." Henrietta and I both gathered the gossip—stuff like who went to Denver to visit relatives, or who was having a fish fry. Not a whole lot was happening in town, much less the ski area, back in the 1960s.

In 1968 the Crested Butte Publishing Company, composed of George Sibley and Don Bachman, both former ski patrolmen, and Art Norris, Western State College professor, whose wife, Bea, ran the Fondue House restaurant, purchased the *Chronicle.* The office was a back room in Don's bar. George served as the editor until he moved with his wife and child to Gothic, handing off the paper to Morgan Queal the week I married Bill in August 1971. She edited it until its sale to Myles Arber.

The *Chronicle* continued to be printed at B&B Printers in Gunnison, thirty miles south. Owned by Fred Budy and his partner and brother-in-law, Bruce Bye, the print shop was the only place in the county where you could get menus, brochures, or just about anything printed, including our one-page flyer, the *Butte Pilot.*

"So . . . ," I asked Fred while I was waiting for the *Butte Pilot* to dry before going into the folder. "Do you think Bill and I would have a chance publishing a competing newspaper?"

     PARENTING A NEWSPAPER

Henrietta Raines in her hair salon, As You Like It, in 1980.

Instead of an answer, Fred launched into a diatribe about Myles Arber's latest transgression in the sanctum sanctorum of the B&B Printers back shop.

"I went out for lunch at noon. And when I returned, he had spread his papers and greasy hamburger all over my desk! It was disgusting."

Tall and hefty, with rarely tamed bushy auburn hair and an unkempt beard, Myles habitually strolled into the Crested Butte Bakery in his brown bathrobe and slippers to buy his morning croissant and coffee.

Fred was a slender, easy going, and fastidious person. Generous with most things, he hated for anyone to disturb his desk.

Returning to my question, he simmered down a bit and regarded me.

"Sure, Sandy. Give it a try. I'll print it for you, too."

Having received Fred's blessing, Bill and I got busy. In November 1972, we morphed the *Butte Pilot* ad flyer into the *Crested Butte Pilot* newspaper on an old rolltop desk my mom had purchased from a long-time Crested Butte resident. From the living room of 422 Elk Avenue, where we were then living, I pounded out stories on the Selectric typewriter from my college days. At age twenty-four, I wasn't far removed from my senior year at the University of Colorado, where I'd been on the *Colorado Daily* newspaper staff.

While I was writing articles and selling ads, Bill converted the old Alphabet building on Elk Avenue into a newspaper office. False-fronted, one story, only twelve and one half feet wide, with faded, painted red wood siding, it was dwarfed by its neighbors, Frank and Gal's Restaurant and Bar on one side and the Grubstake Bar on the other. Starting life during the early 1900s as Rudy Kochevar's barbershop, it served as the combined office of the ski corporation, Crested Butte, Ltd., and the *Chronicle* in the 1960s.

Bill had his work cut out for him, and I was banned from the building so he didn't have to listen to me nit-pick. First he gutted the front half of the place so he could insulate and hang dry wall. During the process, he found tattered newspapers from the early 1900s

The Crested Butte Pilot *Building in 1976 with my wheels in front.*

stuffed in the walls. Quite fitting for a newspaper office, I thought. After reading their papers, the old-timers used them for insulating against the cold, not wrapping fish as the traditional joke goes.

Next Bill divided the space into a front office and a darkroom—my first with running water—although the pipes froze occasionally. Later I would learn how to squeeze into the crawl space and thaw them with a lamp and hair dryer. The tiny area behind the darkroom was jam-packed with a five-foot-long, 500-pound electric addressing machine, complete with foot pedals. Bill ran the machine at first, as he had promised, and when he was consumed with the construction business, a junior high school student addressed the paper to an ever-growing subscriber list of about five hundred. The rear of the building was rented as a small apartment. My sister lived there, as would I in later years.

The most charming part of the office was the front door with its two antique, arched windowpanes providing a perfect view of Stefanic's Grocery across the street and everyone walking by. If I needed some information, I'd wait until the person I wanted to talk to passed in front of the window. Then I'd step outside and corral him or her with questions.

     PARENTING A NEWSPAPER

Martin (Teeny) Tezak in 1980—one of the Pilot's first and most loyal subscribers.

The place became a dropping-in stop for my friends. They knew they could anonymously contribute to the gossip column—social column, that is—headlined "Rambling Babs."

Usually my day was filled with ferreting out stories, typing them up, and sending them down to Fred and Bruce at B&B Printers to be typed into a linotype machine. As soon as I had ten or twelve stories ready, I sealed them in an envelope marked boldly on the front "B&B PRINTERS, 220 SPENCER, GUNNISON, 641-2672. IMPORTANT!! URGENT!!" On the back I drew a small map. Then I hopped on my bicycle, pedaled to the edge of Crested Butte, and waited for a car to stop at my outstretched thumb. Then, instead of jumping into the front seat, I'd thrust the envelope at the startled driver.

"Would you mind dropping this off on your way into Gunnison? It's only one block off the highway. It's copy for the *Crested Butte Pilot.* It's urgent! I'm on deadline."

"Uh, I guess so."

Computers were years down the road. The typewritten stories were originals, with no copies, so if they were lost, we had to start over from scratch, using our notes to rewrite the story. Therefore, I only entrusted the envelope to people I knew, which proved to be a wise choice. One day Don Bachman drove into Gunnison and right through it without stopping at B&B Printers to drop off the envelope. He was almost to Montrose before realizing his omission. Like a true friend, he stood by the side of the road at the edge of Montrose, and just as I had hitchhiked the envelope with him, he hitchhiked the precious cargo with another unsuspecting driver going back to Gunnison.

An expert linotype machine operator, Fred Budy occasionally took the liberty of correcting a misspelling in a story as he typed. Sitting at the tall linotype that held a reservoir of silver-colored molten lead, he punched the correct keys, and a line of type dropped into a metal casing by his arm. When the completed story, now in metal, was sitting in the case, he took it to another machine and sawed off the edges. Each metal line that dropped, accompanied by the punching of the keys, gave off a clickity clackity sound, something I'll always remember even if I've forgotten all the print-shop terminology.

Fred took me under his wing, giving me my own pica pole, a metal ruler measuring

Don Bachman, owner of Tony's Tavern,
later renamed the Wooden Nickel.

   PARENTING A NEWSPAPER

picas and points on one edge and inches on the other; and a make-up rule, a thin, square metal tool that fit snugly into the first three fingers and thumb of my hand. We each used our make-up rule to scrape the bottom of the column of type free from metal fragments before putting the column in the steel page form—literally "making up the page."

Headlines were handset with larger ornate typefaces kept in cabinets, called "California style cases," with shallow pullout trays. Each one had ninety-four square partitions that held the twenty-six letters of the alphabet, upper and lower case, plus punctuation marks and spaces. Take about fifteen different fonts in sizes tiny to huge and you've got a wall-length of cabinets with shallow trays filled with hundreds, maybe thousands of pieces of type.

Bruce Bye was the speed demon of hand setting. A tall, white-haired fatherly type, he'd hold his metal frame in one hand and pull out the letter he needed with the other, his beefy but nimble fingers darting from one little partition to another, and placing each letter against the next. A metal ruler held it all together until he set the headline in the page form above the linotyped story. The lines of type and headlines were made tight against one another, and the whole page was bolted together and readied for the rollers of the press.

Instead of just waiting around for the paper to be printed each week, I actually helped with the physical layout. The newspaper was printed on a heavy white stock, giving it a classy look.

We published the *Pilot* during a period of intense growth for the county and Crested Butte, covering the incorporation of the ski area into the Town of Mt. Crested Butte. We were growing along with the towns, taking part in other "firsts" in the 1970s. Bill's sister and I were cast in the first Mountain Theatre production, *Dark of the Moon,* in the summer of 1972. I wrote about the $100,000 grant that had been won by the town's first planner and his firm, Myles Rademan and BKR Associates, to pave Elk Avenue for the first time in recent history. The planners were also instrumental in guiding the town to form the Board of Zoning and Architectural Review, which I dubbed BOZAR in my editorials and stories. Bill served as its second chairman.

Owning the *Pilot* had finally allowed me to develop my black-and-white photography skills. This was long before the days of color photos in newspapers. And several of my photographs and stories won prizes over the years, including one of the Union Congregational Church, and a portrait of old-timer Fritz Kochevar that I took at Frank and Gal's. I even won an award from the Colorado Press Women's Association—"Best Newspaper edited by a Woman." Actually the *Pilot* was just about the *only* newspaper edited by a woman in our circulation category.

We vied with the *Chronicle* for the lucrative legal publications contracts, both for the new town and for Crested Butte. The legals are those boring notices about meetings and foreclosures in the back pages of a newspaper set in six-point type that take a magnifying glass to read. More expensive than normal display advertising, they are also paid for *on time* by the government agency purchasing them, resulting in dependable revenue even during off-season.

Crested Butte's first aerial weekend in 1975 produced an award-winning photograph—
balloons hovering at the base of Crested Butte Mountain during a misty morning.

Each year the town council accepted bids for a new contract. The winner proudly displayed "The Official Newspaper of Record" imprinted on its masthead, a distinction that Myles Arber was not going to give up without a fight.

All set to bid that first year, we were devastated to discover that the *Pilot* had to be an "official" newspaper, mailed out at second-class postal rates for a full uninterrupted year, before even being eligible to bid. The newspaper was only six months old at the time, so it would be quite a while before we got our chance. In November 1973, we threw ourselves a doozy of a first birthday party—champagne, beer, and a hundred people crammed into the front of the tiny office. The next morning the place reeked of booze, but we had achieved "official newspaper" status and could bid on the coveted legal notices.

No one was sure if Myles had ever argued a case in a courtroom, but every year as the contract came due, he'd buttonhole each council member privately and play prosecuting

 PARENTING A NEWSPAPER

attorney, assuring them that the *Chronicle* was the oldest newspaper in the county and the most widely read.

"*The Pilot* is an ad flyer," he sneered. And pushing his glasses back up his long nose, he cast me a thin-lipped smirk across the aisle of the council meeting room.

One year we underbid him and still the council gave him the contract. It set the stage for bitter rivalry in all areas. And more than once I came home in tears.

Losing the contract was not the worst thing that could happen to us. In the meantime more writing and photo awards lay ahead, including one for "Best News Story" I wrote after the building next door to the *Pilot* office burned down, almost taking us with it.

After delivering newspapers at the ski area that cold, overcast Friday, I started to drive back down the hill when I saw an enormous cloud of smoke rising in the early morning of December 13, 1974.

Approaching Elk Avenue, I realized the smoke was emanating from somewhere close to my office. The fire engine—a 1950s-era pumper truck, not the high-performance vehicles the fire department has today—had already arrived. Smoke was pouring from the eaves of Frank and Gal's, a historic structure that the Starikas recently had sold to Don Waldrop and Alfredo and Nidia Villanueva, who operated Sancho's Mexican Restaurant there. Wind was blowing the smoke toward the *Pilot* office, a mere eighteen feet away.

I dashed into the office and started collecting stuff—just in case, mind you. I figured the fire boys would have it extinguished before the flames got out of hand. We had covered the founding of the first Crested Butte Fire Protection District in 1973, and knew the volunteers had top-notch training and even uniforms. Bill was a member. However, they liked to joke that "we've never lost a lot."

A friend offered to carry my photo enlarger to his darkroom in the Company Store. I shrugged off his offer at first. Then I did a double take and saw the flames licking the window frames of the restaurant. The heat had already broken the glass. He carried the enlarger like a baby down the street to safety.

Next to the subscription files and enlarger, my most precious treasure was my photo negative collection from the past six years. I gathered them all in their little wooden boxes to lock in my car. More friends took what I hastily shoved at them to their shops or nearby homes. "Are your old-timer photos still on the walls at Frank

Frank and Gal's Restaurant and Bar in 1974,
home of Gal's famous ravioli.

The volunteer firefighters man the hose at the rear of Frank and Gal's.

and Gal's?" they asked. Luckily I had taken them down after the sale to the Villanuevas and they resided in my safety deposit box.

The marshal threw open the door. "OK, Sandy. That's it. Outta here!"

"Kemp, just let me pack up a few more things. Then I'll leave, I promise."

"Sandy, if you don't get out of here right now, I'm going to have to arrest you."

A soft spoken, almost apologetic threat—but he meant it and he was my friend, so after one last look and one last grab, I retreated to the sidewalk in front of Stefanic's. The street became an ice rink watered by the fire hoses stretching over Elk Avenue like gray snakes. I hunched up in my jacket against the cold and fear, a cigarette dangling from my fingers, a furrow of worry creasing my forehead. Three firemen sat on a hose directed at the west side of my office, soaking the old dry wood to keep it from spontaneously combusting as the flames grew higher and hotter. Frank and Gal's finally collapsed with a blazing flare-up and blast of heat that cracked the windows and blistered the paint of the buildings across the street.

Hours later, as the pile of rubble smoldered, I returned to my office. A chaotic mess, with the inside of some walls scorched and the outside walls slightly charred, it had survived.

Aside from that close call, things went along swimmingly for a while. We were running eight pages a week, having started with four to six. Trying to ease my load, I hired a series of part-time employees. In 1977, B&B Printers, along with most of the rest of the publishing world, began switching over to "cold type" or offset, replacing the "hot type" letterpress process of the linotype machine. The stories were typed into a machine that printed them out onto glossy paper. Cut into columns, they were waxed on the back to make them sticky, and pasted onto the layout sheet, which was then photographed. A plate was burned from the negative and attached to the press. Much of the layout procedure was done in the newspaper office, with only the finished pages traveling to the print shop.

While I was busy at the layout table relearning cutting and pasting from my kindergarten years, plus attending to all the details of the newspaper business, Bill quit holding up his end with the billing and bookkeeping chores. Or maybe I gradually took them away from him. His construction business was his thing and the newspaper mine, and well—to make it short, we got divorced.

The *Pilot* then became my obsession and my albatross. Like Frank and Gal's building, I was on the way to a major burnout. I developed a skin rash.

Shortly after I put out the word that I wanted to sell the whole shooting match, Myles Arber skulked over late one winter night—I was living in the back of the building by then. Reluctantly I let him inside.

"I want to buy the *Pilot* and the building," he announced without preamble.

"Why?" I sat on the other side of the narrow room as far away from him as I could get.

"Simple, to buy out the competition." He snickered nervously. His high-pitched New York City voice grated on me.

I was mildly flattered to hear him finally admit we were competition after years of referring to the *Pilot* as a throwaway gossip sheet. But it was obvious the real estate in the middle of the Elk Avenue business district would be most valuable for him. His office was on a back street, not conducive to walk-in news. My stomach turned over at the thought of selling out to him, of giving up and letting down all the people who had supported the *Pilot* for four years with news, subscriptions, ads, and shoulders to cry on. On top of that he was involved in four libel suits.

"Forget it."

On Valentine's Day 1977, I sat in a chair at Jean Paul's Coiffures.

"Oh, Jean Paul. What am I going to do? I gotta get out from under this newspaper. It's not fun anymore. My marriage is kaput . . . and look at this rash on my arms."

He snipped away as I babbled, finally announcing in his French accent, "Zee hairs, they are cut." And he whipped off the plastic cape around my shoulders with a flourish.

"Why don't you and Suzanne come to the party tomorrow," I asked as I paid him. "I sold the *Pilot* building and we're all tapping a keg to celebrate. Unfortunately they didn't want the newspaper. You can buy it if you want."

We both laughed. But I didn't rule out the idea. He and a partner had started Le Bosquet, a fancy French restaurant. Jean Paul was multi-talented and possibly deep-pocketed.

"It would give Suzanne something to do," he mused.

Suzanne, his girlfriend, a gorgeous, slender blonde, gave manicures and pedicures in Jean Paul's salon. Picture the mid-1970s, hippies filtering into Crested Butte, residents holding two and three jobs—do you see anyone paying for a manicure?

"Jean Paul, not only will it give her something to do, it will totally consume her life." I was trying to warn him, but at the same time yearning for a faint glimmer of hope at the end of my long, black tunnel.

Suzanne came by three hours later with an offer and a request to look at the books. My rash stopped itching. I sold the *Pilot* for a pittance two days later to Jean Paul Simille and his partner, Ted Hoeller, who ran the CBS Disco across the street. Finally I was out—but I was poor.

Ted's wife, Sharon, ran the paper with Suzanne, while I stayed on as the photographer and adviser. It took about a year for Suzanne and Jean Paul to break up. She and Sharon ran it for a few months before it was sold to Lee and Jane Ervin and a group of friends from the Midwest. Then Jane and Lee split up and their *Pilot* and Myles Arber's *Chronicle* merged in April 1985. I took a photo of Lee, Jane, and Myles, arms around each other, for the front-page announcement. I was photographing for the *Chronicle* by then, Lee and I having butted heads once too often. Myles finally realized he was better off publishing the paper from afar, so we rarely crossed paths.

Sandy Fails, who became the editor of the new *Crested Butte Chronicle and Pilot,* was a joy to work with. She actually has a journalism degree, the only one among all the editors I've worked with.

Despite the stress of the *Pilot,* I never could fully exit the newspaper world—the variety, meeting new people, shooting photos, covering events; I loved that. My full-page photo features were common. I wrote a regular column on mountain living, a social column that we dubbed "Grapevine," and a softball column. It was an exciting and creative time. By then the paper had gone high-tech with new Apple computers. But the pay was still as lousy as ever—$40 a week.

The milestone of my fortieth birthday provoked me into examining my life—where I'd been and where I was going, and of special interest, will I have any money when I get there? The *Mountain Sun,* the Crested Butte publication of the *Gunnison Country Times,* came to my rescue in 1986. For the first time in my life I had full-time newspaper work with full-time pay and even some benefits. I joined an experienced four-person staff. To my great delight, they gave me almost free rein with photo spreads and feature stories. So I was not prepared in 1991 to be laid off. Deeply disappointed, I tried to open myself to new directions. Re-married two years previously and wanting to stay that way, I was even a bit relieved to never have to sit through another council meeting or stay up until one a.m. to photograph the Red Lady Ball.

At the *Chronicle and Pilot,* meanwhile, editors came and went, and finally the new, young staff members bought out the owners in August 2000 and renamed the paper the *Crested Butte News.* They relegated the *Chronicle and Pilot* logo to miniscule type at the top of the nameplate.

 PARENTING A NEWSPAPER

Dropping by their office one day, I happened across one of the old wooden newspaper display boxes Bill had built for the *Pilot*. Picking it up, I turned around to tell someone its history, but all the someones, half of whom I didn't even know, were intently staring at computer screens, fingers flying. Instead of hitchhiking down to Gunnison, the stories were zooming over the wires. And I smiled at the thought of my typewriter, now considered an antique.

I use my forty years of Gunnison County newspapering experience to write for magazines now—my own stories and other people's. And if you are reading this book then I guess Bill did me a favor when he said, "We can start a newspaper."

CHAPTER 6

If Stefanic's Don't Have It, You Don't Need It

Tony Stefanic sweeps snow off the sidewalk in front of his grocery in 1976.

$\mathcal{S}$TEFANIC'S WAS THE ONLY GROCERY in town in the late 1960s. Whether you lived at the ski area or in Crested Butte, if you ran out of milk before the weekly trek to the Safeway in Gunnison and to visit the laundromat, you went to Stefanic's on Elk Avenue in the heart of Crested Butte.

The tall false-fronted building was a small-town conglomerate: grocery store, soda fountain, drugstore, newsstand, butcher, and hardware, all under one roof. A modest sign in the lower right-hand window told you it was "Stefanic's General Store." A larger sign hanging over the front door read "Tony's Grocery," and underneath, "Coca-Cola." Whether you called it Tony's, Stefanic's, or just the grocery store, everyone knew what you meant.

Hand-lettered cardboard signs inside the front windows announced all that the store had to offer, including, during the fall, klobassi (klobase) sausage, a Slavic specialty. In hunting season, the window display featured bright, Day-Glo orange hats and vests. Just inside the door, a rack of sun-faded postcards stood near the magazines. Eleanor Stefanic's rolltop desk where she figured the tabs was in the northwest corner. Near it were wooden cubbyholes for the *Denver Post* for down-valley ranchers. To the right was the ice cream/milkshake corner. The oiled pine plank floor stretched back past tall glass cases cluttered with sundries, and shelves of cereals and canned goods. Snow shovels and coal buckets decorated the rear walls rising to a 16-foot-high wainscoted ceiling. The potbelly coal stove was opposite the butcher department.

Stefanic's carried many items, but all of them were high priced.

"It's the freight" was the usual excuse. However, it was well-known that Tony Stefanic knew how to hang onto a dollar bill. The local rumor was that Tony hid his money in coffee cans in the basement. I thought there was only coal down there. I had seen it loaded off the truck, slid through a chute into the basement window. But I was wrong. Many years later Rudy Sedmak, a contemporary of Tony's, confirmed the rumor. He'd seen the cans of silver dollars.

Stefanic's big claim to fame was steak. Since nightlife was a bit rare in the late 1960s, the best a guy might do to court his honey was offer to buy two thick steaks from Stefanic's, bring them over, and let her cook them. He usually provided the beer or wine and the bigger part of the appetite.

These steaks didn't come on a Styrofoam tray, wrapped in plastic, dated, and price-stickered like today's supermarket meat. No siree. These babies were hand-cut by Tony himself.

Once you decided to splurge, a trip was made to the back corner of Stefanic's. Tony, in his white, slightly-soiled-around-the-waist apron, presided over the wooden butcher block on a carpet of clean sawdust from Rozman's sawmill up the street.

"What'll it be?" he asked.

T-bone, of course, and as long as you'd made this expensive culinary decision, steaks an inch and one-half thick were de rigueur.

Tony disappeared into the back walk-in cooler and returned carrying a giant slab of beef in his arms like a baby. He laid it tenderly on the block, wiped it with a clean white towel, and selected a tool from his array of cleavers—a knife the size of a samurai sword. "How thick did you say?"

"Inch and a half."

Tony laid the sword gently across the meat, eyeballing a generous inch and half. "How's that?"

He gave you a chance to change your mind.

"Well, it is a special occasion. Maybe just a teensy bit more."

"How's this?"

"Perfect!"

The sword slipped easily through the dark red meat. When the bone stopped it, Tony reached for the large bowsaw hanging by a nail on the wall.

Following the surgery, he wiped the steaks with a fresh cloth, slapped them on a piece of white butcher paper, weighed them on his large, shiny white scale, wrapped them up, and tied white string around the package. He marked the price on the top with a black grease pencil before retreating to his butcher block to sharpen the sword.

At the counter, Tony's wife, Eleanor, deciphered the black scribble and took that precious $10 bill. She tapped the price into the old black adding machine, pulled down the long handle, figured the tax, and gave you the bit of tape as a receipt and, if you were fortunate, some change. If you were on their tab list, she wrote it down on a receipt pad. Almost everyone in town had a tab.

I can't recall the price per pound. I know the steaks were expensive, but it was sure cheaper than eating out at a restaurant. What I do remember is how delicious they were, accompanied by a bottle of red wine from Yelenicks' Liquor Store, and sautéed wild mushrooms.

ELEANOR, now an active eighty-four-year-old, easily recalls memories of her life as one-half of Stefanic's Grocery.

Born in Ripley County, Indiana, Eleanor Carolyn Hardebeck was from German stock. Many of her relatives originally settled in Cincinnati, where she worked at the Western Electric Telephone Company. On a train ride from Cincinnati in the early 1940s, Eleanor, the only person in the coach, was quietly reading a book.

"All the servicemen were supposed to be on the car behind. Suddenly this sailor comes into the coach and asks me if the seat next to me is taken. He sat down. I kept on reading, but he kept talking. He really irritated me. Finally I slammed the book shut and asked, 'Now what do you want?!' He replied, 'Would you mind writing to a lonely sailor?'"

Eleanor and Tony corresponded for a couple of years, while their love blossomed. She laughs recounting the time he came to visit her.

Eleanor Stefanic takes time out over the coffee cans in 1987.

"The Ohio River had flooded, as it often did, overflowing the streets. And Tony had to roll up his pant legs, carry his shoes, and wade to my house."

When Eleanor was twenty-four, Tony brought her to his home in Crested Butte.

"It was beautiful! Of course it was—it was August, and we came over Kebler Pass, where I saw my first deer."

Wed in Indiana on December 1, 1945, the young couple bought the general store, built in 1874, from John and Fanny Byouk, and opened for business in January 1946.

"Before the Byouks' time it was Mike Fisher's pool hall, with one side for the ladies, where they sipped apple cider, and the other side for the men, who shot pool and drank beer. Upstairs was a dance hall with red velvet rugs and drapes. At one time there was also a millinery shop upstairs. I donated the cider press to the Crested Butte Museum," said Eleanor.

"Tony told me stories about how they drilled holes in the floor, plugged with cork, to let the spilled beer run through. The bartenders wore cleats on their boots to keep their feet dry and so they wouldn't slip on the beer. Fisher's reputation was that 'they wasted more beer than the other bars sold.'

"They used to deliver beer barrels into the basement with a team of horses, entering from the back under the porch," she added.

The Stefanics kept the potbelly stove fired up night and day. "Everyone liked to come in our store because the other stores were so cold," recalled Eleanor.

Stefanic's was open from 7:30 a.m. to six p.m. Monday through Saturday and for several hours Sunday morning so people could pick up their morning *Denver Post* and *Rocky Mountain News.* Most evenings, it was 7:30 by the time she got done with the bookwork and Tony finished cleaning up the butcher shop. At last the weary couple could climb the stairs to their apartment over the store.

"We tried to close earlier, but people kept coming in, " said Eleanor.

During their precious Sunday afternoons they sometimes went for a drive in their blue Ford Bronco.

In the early days their competitors were the CF&I Company Store, located in today's Company Store building at Third Street and Elk Avenue, and John's Store, a few doors east, owned by John Sporcich. Tony learned the business from George Spehar, previous owner of John's Store, by starting as a delivery boy. Many of Stefanic's customers were women who had come to America from Slavic countries like Croatia and Slovenia and couldn't speak English. Tony's Slovenian mother didn't speak English either. Eleanor remembered with a tinge of sadness how left out she felt when they always wanted Tony to wait on them because he could speak Slavic.

"Plus I was second-generation German and it was right after the war . . ."

The Byouk daughters, Clara Niccoli and Pauline Gallowich, befriended Eleanor.

"I used to be a great cake baker at home. But here instead of rising, the middle always fell on me, so Pauline showed me how to bake them at this altitude. I also had a terrible time with fires. Growing up I had lived in a big, old brick house, which was heated with gas. I didn't realize you had to keep adding coal or wood. I thought the fire would keep on going like gas did once it was lit." She laughed. "Crested Butte was quite a change for me."

Back in those days, the store carried a little bit of everything and then some. Eleanor smiled as she repeated a slogan someone told her: "If Stefanic's don't have it, you don't need it."

Stefanic's was the only place in town where you could buy ice cream cones. Near the front window of the store was a small cooler, covered with black rubber lids. Inside were cardboard gallon containers of vanilla, chocolate, and strawberry ice cream.

Once in a while an imaginative flavor showed up, no doubt pressed upon Stefanic's by a desperate supplier. I came from the city, spoiled by Baskin Robbins 31 Flavors, especially licorice. So vanilla, chocolate, and strawberry held little appeal for me. The summer afternoon I discovered "licorice ice cream" hand-lettered on the cardboard sign over the cooler,

The Company Store, in 1975, across the street from Stefanic's, is flanked by Yelenicks' Liquor Store and the Masonic Hall, which would later house the Senior Citizens Center.

I was ecstatic. So was Eleanor. I think until she heard my exclamation of delight she was convinced she would be stuck with licorice until January. For my quarter, she loaded a generous scoop onto my cone—equal to three regular scoops. The resulting mountain of ice cream was a bit precarious, so I sat on a bench outside the store until I could lick it down to walking size.

Someone stopped and ogled the black ice cream. "Where'd you get that?"

"Inside." I pointed.

The person emerged from the store minutes later with a cone almost, but not quite, as large as mine. Someone else stopped by the bench.

"Where did you get that black ice cream?"

"Through that door." I pointed again.

The cone that appeared a couple minutes later was smaller still. By the time I returned to the store for another licorice fix several days later, the cones were back to their normal one-scoop size. I guess Eleanor figured that licorice had some sales potential after all.

Besides the ice cream and milkshakes—chocolate and vanilla were the local favorites, not licorice, which never appeared again—they stocked a Brach's candy rack, and postcards of local scenes, most of them shot by Eleanor.

"I learned to use a camera in Cincinnati and I loved to photograph. We introduced post-cards to Gunnison County," she said. "Of course, we had to order ten thousand of them in order to keep the price at a nickel a piece.

"We also took orders from Crested Butte families for coal and cattle saltlicks. After the Crested Butte mines closed, the Somerset mine would deliver coal here for the individual families, who would pay us."

And because it was always "coming next Friday" at Tony Mihelich's Crested Butte Hardware, the Stefanics carried assorted hardware supplies, including house paint, linoleum rugs, kitchen ranges (that you had to order in advance, of course), coal buckets, snow shovels, and hunting and fishing gear.

"We had rock specimens from the different mines around that we sold for souvenirs, and the ski area let us use their logo on the sweatshirts we sold. We were the first to sell sweatshirts here."

And always, before the age of vegetarians, the meat.

Stefanic's window told you what was happening in town and available in the store.
In 1987, homemade sausage got top billing.

"When I first started, I couldn't tell the difference between beef and pork, but it didn't take me long," Eleanor remembered.

While Tony was having surgery in Denver in the early 1980s, the petite, blonde Eleanor asked her customers to carry the heavy sides of meat from the back cooler to the butcher block where she cut them.

"Once Gary Garcia (owner of the Idle Spur next door to Stefanic's) came in to get some steaks and ended up cutting for all the customers," she recalled fondly.

Life in her newly adopted small town was not easy for Eleanor. She voiced a typical woman's complaint. "There was no place to shop for clothes. I weighed 102 pounds and wore a size 7 [equivalent to today's size 2]. The smallest size in the CF&I Supply Store in the Company Store was a size 12. So I made most of my clothes."

And when her daughters, Marcia and Rose, and son, Marty, came along, she sewed all their clothes as well; this in addition to shoveling snow from the steep, narrow wooden back stairs to their second-floor apartment.

"It snowed almost daily, and I did the back while Tony took care of the front." Before the town took over the snowplowing, each shopkeeper shoveled the snow from in front of his business.

The closing of the coal mines in the 1950s, putting most miners out of work, only made life harder for the Stefanics. "We did a lot of credit business. When people sold their homes and left town, they gave us their addresses, and I billed them and they paid when they could. The poorer ones paid first.

"After all the businesses closed down, the town was held together by Yelenicks' Liquor Store, Frank and Gal's, Tony's Hardware, the post office, Willard Ruggera working by himself over at Town Hall, and us at the store."

Just about the time the ex-miners paid up, the Chapter 11 bankruptcy of the ski area owner in the late 1960s forced the Stefanics to carry more people on credit. Throughout the 1970s other problems emerged. When the town's water pipes froze during the "Winter of No Snow," 1977–1978, the family carried water from Coal Creek and had to draw drinking water from a spring at Niccoli's Ranch down the valley.

Eleanor remembered feeling very tied down by the store. "I was pretty much married to it. I felt like I was carrying a counter on my shoulder."

Occasionally they had part-time help. June Krizmanich was a loyal employee for seventeen years, and as the children grew up, they, too, helped wait on customers and scoop ice cream.

Once, Eleanor was instrumental in catching a woman passing counterfeit money.

"I handled so much money, I could just tell that the [bill] didn't feel right. I gave a description of a woman from Chicago who had given me the twenty-dollar bill, and the cops caught her." Eleanor has an incredible memory for detail, but she said with a smile, "I try to forget the bad things."

The one bad thing she never forgot was being robbed in 1975, while Tony was away having surgery.

Pete Raines in 1969, retired miner and father to my friend Henrietta,
was one of the few who stayed in town after the mines closed.

June Krizmanich asked me to photograph her and John on their 38th wedding anniversary in 1980.

"They came upstairs in the middle of the night after breaking the front window. They got me out of bed and held me at gunpoint. They tried to make me open the safe, but I said, 'I don't know how.'

"'We know that you know how to open the safe.'"

"So I said, 'I can't see to open it without my glasses.' They marched me right upstairs to get my glasses. They had also cut the telephone lines. I could smell liquor on their breath. One was wearing a ski mask, and the other had a white sheet with eyeholes. I was determined when they opened the front door to leave I would run across to the Grubstake, bathrobe and all. But I realized it was 4:30 a.m. and no one would be around."

After the robbers hightailed it through the back door with the two thousand dollars from the safe, she crept next door to the Gamble's Store, where she woke up owners Steve and Rosemary Smith, who lived upstairs. They called the police to track the robbers through thirteen inches of snow. This was before the town had a bank and residents could make daily deposits. No way Stefanic's made two thousand dollars that day in ice cream and steaks.

Marshal Rob McClung came over right away and, because it was snowing, was able to follow the perpetrators' tracks. He found the bed sheet discarded by the thieves. Then the tracks intersected with others. Rob went home, got his bloodhound Daisy, gave her a whiff of the sheet, and off they went sniffing up to 106 Sopris. One of the suspects, Jim Pickett, split before a search warrant could be issued and was on the lam for six months, with McClung in hot pursuit via the Colorado Bureau of Investigation and the FBI. The other was kept under surveillance for a couple of days before being booked on suspicion of armed robbery. It was hoped he could lead them to the stolen money. It was never recovered, but Eleanor had records of the checks and asked everyone to rewrite them.

To add insult to injury, two weeks later, Stefanic's was jolted by an explosion, possibly caused by a stick of dynamite set off near the garage.

Jim Pickett finally called McClung and told him he was ready to give himself up. But he never appeared. In August, McClung was driving to Gunnison on official business when, as he drove through Almont, he heard a whistle. There was Pickett standing on the side of the road with his thumb out, grinning.

"I told you I would give myself up. It just took a little time to get here."

Eleanor and Tony, glad to see the robbers caught, weren't about to let themselves be scared out of business by the robbery and blast. But age and illness eventually caught up with them. After forty years in the business, Tony hung up the samurai sword for good on December 31, 1985, and they locked the front door for the last time. Lifting boxes, butchering sides of beef, and now diabetes had taken their toll. The children, long gone, didn't want to take over the business. Newly opened, modern McDell's Grocery, the Takeaway, and the Marketplace were stiff competition.

Stefanic's closed. During their final six months, sixty-four-year-old Eleanor ran the business by herself.

The hand-lettered signs came down, and the empty windows got dustier and dustier. Tony and Eleanor retreated upstairs. She took walks, visited friends, and drove Tony around in their Bronco. In 1988, and again in 1992 and 2000, the building was leased. No one could make a go of it. Year by year Tony's health declined, and after his death on January 31, 1994, Eleanor moved to Gunnison.

"I didn't like being alone all the time. And Marty, my son, lives there."

One day Eleanor grabbed me in a parking lot. "I sold it! I sold the store! Cash deal." I had never seen her so excited. And little wonder. Insurance costs and property taxes were wearing her down. I was pleased for her. Those silver dollars from the basement had to be long spent.

She didn't know the new owner's plans for the building, but to me, Stefanic's would never be the same without Tony and his samurai sword.

Eleanor has blossomed in Gunnison, volunteering at the Young at Hearts and the Gunnison Pioneer Museum. She often comes to Crested Butte for holidays like Memorial Day. "Tony wasn't happy unless he was moving. I'm the same. Even to this day, I have trouble sitting down. I need to be doing something. I still miss the store and interacting with people."

The building is undergoing major rehabilitation. The owners donated Tony's white butcher scale and the family's piano to the Crested Butte Mountain Heritage Museum.

CHAPTER 7

Memorial Day

A uniformed John Krizmanich is ready to march in the 1980 Memorial Day parade.

C RESTED BUTTE'S MEMORIAL DAY celebration is not intended to impress tourists or rake in revenues for the town or local businesses. It's a quiet, eloquent tribute to family and community—a simple marching parade of military veterans to the cemetery, where Mass is celebrated, followed by a march back into town and a rip-roaring polka party.

The veterans had been making the march for about fifty years by the time I first began attending in 1971 to cover the event for the *Crested Butte Pilot*. I was a little late to the party, and the exact start time of the parade was something I never could keep straight year after year.

"Martha," I asked my next door-neighbor, "When does the parade start?"

"Well, I know Mass starts at eleven. I'll go ask Whitey [Sporcich, her husband]. He's handing out the bullets this year because Jake can't make it."

Whitey's answer was pretty vague. So I'd ask Marlene Stajduhar at the post office, whose husband, Sonny, carried one of the flags.

"Marlene, any idea what time the parade starts?"

"Well, I think around nine-thirty or so," she replied.

I'd ride my bicycle uptown, like all locals did at the time, somewhere around nine, and I almost always made it on time.

Now, as then, the Crested Butte veterans, mostly of World War II and Korean War vintage, gather outside the Old Town Hall with their families and close friends. Some live in Crested Butte; others come from their homes scattered around Gunnison County. The men make small talk and joke about the snug fit of their cleaned, pressed uniforms, decorated with combat ribbons, medals, and name bars. They greet each other with bear hugs, hearty handshakes, and laughter; it's been a year since many last saw each other. The Veterans of the Foreign Wars (VFW) Post commander hands out white marine-style helmets to those without uniforms, and the rifles and three bullets to each of the men bearing arms for the salute at the cemetery.

Soon the bantering dies down. It is time. For more than twenty-five years, the late Martin "Pitsker" Sporcich, detail commander, ordered the men to "fall in" when it looked like they were all there. All ten to fifteen of them, or as in 1976, all five of them. And he marched beside them barking orders. When his legs began to fail, he reluctantly accepted a ride. But he always stood ramrod straight as he sent the men on their way, his voice having weathered time better than his legs.

His successor is Donald Tucker, Crested Butte's popular bus driver. Tuck, a tall, slender gentleman, showed up for his first Memorial Day around 1988. One of the few Vietnam vets in the parade, he was given a helmet and marched as proudly as the fifteen others in his Levi jacket, bell-bottomed jeans, and cowboy boots. Today in his camouflage fatigues and

Memorial Day 1995, when more veterans than usual marched in the rain past the Old Town Hall.
Tuck is third from right in camouflage.

shiny black combat boots, Tuck orders "fall in!" Halfway down the block he begins counting the cadence in his booming baritone:

"I don't know but I been told

Crested Butte is mighty cold.

Sound off, one two

Sound off, three four

Sound off, one two, one two three four."

The veterans, splendid and solemn in their uniforms, march briskly down Elk Avenue out to the Crested Butte cemetery. All branches of the service are represented in navy blue, olive drab, camouflage fatigues, or dress whites. Sonny Stadjuhar, Johnny Cobai, and Joe Starika, bearing the colors, led them for all the years I worked for the newspapers, never missing a beat as I ran along beside them and jumped in front to shoot photos.

The only sound is the measured rhythm of their boots striking the pavement and the wind whipping the flags—the American, the Crested Butte chapter of the VFW, and the state of Colorado. The biggest and strongest guys are usually the flag bearers. It's not an easy task on a blustery day.

Small knots of people respectfully line Elk Avenue. No one cheers like they do for the festive July Fourth or Flauschink parades. Which makes sense—this is a march, even though the locals call it a "parade." The few tourists, caught by surprise as the men pass, place their hands over their hearts or remove their hats. There is a smattering of applause, which, as the years have gone by, has grown louder.

"Not a lot of fanfare," commented one visitor.

They don't need it. They've got it all inside.

During all the years I've photographed this parade, only the participants have changed as the older men drop out and younger vets step up to take their place in line. In recent years, Vietnam and Gulf War vets have marched. Sometimes we see a few Boy Scouts flanked by a dog or two. Other years we sigh at the absence of those who have died, such as detail commander "Pitsker" and U.S. Navy man Johnny Cobai. In their honor in 1991, the lead car sported a pair of combat boots with the laces tied to a tiny flag on the hood.

I try to get a new angle for whatever publication I'm working for at the time—a long lens, a short one. Close-ups, a faraway shot. I got a very different angle one year. Falling on the last week of May, the day usually offers a tantalizing taste of summer with blue skies, puffy clouds, and dandelions. Not so in 1989, when we were surprised by wind and snow. The folks visiting from warmer parts of Colorado were totally unprepared. The ladies, wearing open-toed sandals, shivered in their spring dresses. I rode my bike to the cemetery behind the parade toasty in my winter jacket, mittens, and a wool ski hat. Many sat out Mass in their cars, watching snowflakes plaster against the priest's white robes.

The marching men are followed at a respectful distance by a slow line of cars carrying friends and relatives. Past the four-way stop, the old soldiers relax, slow their march to a brisk walk—it is about a mile to the cemetery—and chat among themselves.

"Where's the polka party this time?"

"Man, my feet are killing me."

"Wonder if this uniform will still fit next year."

"Did you hear the joke about . . ."

At the cemetery entrance they are again on display. Shoulders back and chests up, they stride up to the chapel. Tuck gives the command to "un ten hut" and they all relax, weapons from over their shoulders leaned up against the side of the chapel.

The cars park along the narrow dirt cemetery road, and their occupants begin a daylong reunion. All the old-time families in Crested Butte are related: the Sporciches, Starikas, Kapushions, Kochevars, Rozmans, Somraks, Sedmaks, Ruggeras, Spritzers, and many more. The visiting relatives from milder climates look forward to catching up on the news and gossip.

In preparation for the day, residents spruced up the cemetery, raking rocks and dead weeds, trying to turn back the inevitable wave of sagebrush that is pulling at pant legs and snagging pantyhose. The Altar and Rosary Society ladies dusted the chapel and laid out clean linen. Martha Sporcich pressed the tiny American flags with which she and Whitey decorated the graves of veterans who no longer have family to care for them. She washed

Assembling for Mass at the cemetery chapel in 1983.

the dusty plastic flowers that had wintered by the graves and hung them on her clothesline to dry.

When I first saw the plastic flowers pinned to our neighbor's clothesline, I was puzzled and almost embarrassed to ask. So I surreptitiously took a photo instead and queried my friend Nettie Kapushion, who filled me in. "It's for all the people who can't make it here to put flowers on the graves." In freshly scrubbed mason jars, the flowers wave with the miniature flags.

The soldiers and friends sit on the edge of the Love and Snellar plots across from the chapel, chewing the fat while they wait for Mass to start. Others walk up the knoll to talk with those who can't talk back, running a slow hand over the engraving in the stone, remembering . . .

During Mass the elderly sit on the two rows of folding chairs—but not very many of them, because no one in Crested Butte likes to think of themselves as old. We start by singing "America the Beautiful." Many take communion. The priest asks remembrance for all who have died the past year. And the names are called out from the audience, one by one—old-timers, new-timers, suicides, and car accident victims. He says a prayer for them all. At the end, led by those of us recruited as a choir, everyone sings "The Battle Hymn of the Republic," always too slowly, but usually all three verses. The hymn is a marching song, not a dirge, so I try to speed it up; the priest smiles and nods his approval at me. Afterwards, we all hug and brush away the tears.

Tuck barks another command, and the detail marches away from the chapel. All face Crested Butte Mountain. The riflemen fire high toward the mountain three times in honor of their fallen comrades. Each one picks up his spent cartridges.

Every year before his death Johnny Cobai pleaded via the local newspapers for a bugler. His sister Darlene played for a while, but in recent years the music had been missing. In 1988 his prayers were answered. An older gentleman from Arizona, who summers here, read the paper. After the three shots, Ken Orrell raised his horn and played an achingly mournful "Taps."

The men march off towards town, the cars following respectfully behind, headed not home but "uptown" for the second half of the Memorial Day—the celebration. All the bars in town at one time or another have hosted the traditional afternoon polka party. The bartender sets up a long table stretching from the front windows to the back corner, where a polka band warms up. All the vets pull up chairs, and pretty soon there are eight beers in front of each as they vie to buy a round for their friends.

Ties are loosened, jackets come off, shirtsleeves are rolled up, and everyone gets down to business. In years past I can remember expert polka dancer Sonny Stadjuhar gracefully whirling his slender Marlene around the cramped floor. Casualness not being his style, he is still wearing his navy hat and jacket. In a little while he takes off his hat, then later sheds his jacket. Elmer Rudeen of Gunnison, in his neatly pressed navy whites, is the next one out. Ladies wait in line for a dance with the best. Willard Ruggera, whose World War II uniform still buttons easily over his middle, smoothly glides across the floor with his wife, Ronnie. Soon we are all swinging, and it seems the music never stops.

Until his death, Botsie Spritzer played his accordion on Memorial Day. Since then it's been the Mraule brothers, or Pete Dunda (after he changes out of his uniform), or the Spritzer brothers from Gunnison, or Chris Rouse, raised in Crested Butte and taught in part by Botsie.

Sonny and Marlene Stajduhar dancing the polka in 1987.
After a while, he'll take off his hat.

These Crested Butte natives, who fought in World War I for different countries, found themselves together at Frank and Gal's in 1968. From left: Emil Lunk, a German soldier under the Kaiser. Frank Hodgson, of English descent; Tony Danni, whose father came from Italy and homesteaded a ranch at Jack's Cabin; John Panian, a Yugoslavian immigrant; and Ralph Falsetto, also of Italian parentage, all fought with the Allies.

Almost everyone knows the words to the polkas—the old-timers sing in Croatian—and they sing loudly, but only one verse, as singing and dancing simultaneously are best left to someone in better physical condition. Some remember more words than others do. But we all shout the final chorus: "I'm telling you, baby, I'm telling you, just because, just because!"

A few of the celebrants used to wander over to the Senior Citizens Center, gone now, to take a break from the beer, smoke, and noise. They sat and drank coffee, visiting and looking at my old-timer photos on the walls, searching for their family members, or suddenly turning to share a story. Today folks drop in at the parish hall of the Queen of All Saints Catholic Church, where some volunteers have organized a potluck lunch with delicious homemade desserts, including, if we're lucky, a povitica. Their only request is a few dollars' donation or a side dish.

Always the talk, easy friendly bantering, smiles, laughter, singing, and—most of all—love. This is the genuine Crested Butte; the Crested Butte pre-ski area, pre-condos, pre-anything but coal mining and ranching. The fabric that is Crested Butte glows.

Former marine Whitey Sporcich sums it up, "We drink beer and reminisce about things that happened forty-five years ago, and then someone packs us home." He throws his head back and laughs. And when his brother Pitsker waves an arthritic fist in the air and hollers above the accordion music, "Is everybody happy?" they are.

CHAPTER 8

Hot and Cold—Heating with Wood

1976–1989

My sister wrestles a truckload of wood in the driveway of her new home in 1977, ready to be cut into rounds and split. The white house behind her burned down from a chimney fire.

"**H**ANK AND I ARE MOVING TO HOTCHKISS," read the note from my younger sister. "We need you to buy my house. Dinner tonight at seven. We'll talk."

Kathleen purchased her house at 512 Sopris in 1976, several years prior to meeting her husband Hank. She'd given me a tour before making her big leap. A small log structure, it had an old gas Heatilator as its only heat source, attached to the drafty living room wall, adjacent to the kitchen. Beyond the kitchen was a small bathroom with a wooden toilet seat and a large tub. Upstairs were two bedrooms, and out back a rickety shed that she wanted to convert into her pottery studio.

The previous renters were Pres and Judy Pitta, owners of the Warming House at the ski area. Someone—maybe Pres—had done some remodeling of the kitchen, or, judging from the age of the house, "modeling" of the kitchen. A tin pie plate covered the hole where the stovepipe had connected with a coal cook stove, now replaced with a four-burner gas range. The unusually low Formica countertops were red. Judy was a small woman. Kathy wasn't too tall either, so they were a fit. I walked through the dusty entry with its peeling wallpaper and shook my head. "It needs a lot of work, Kathy."

Ignoring my opinion as usual, she plunked down money for the first major investment of her life, then installed a new state-of-the-art Vermont Castings Defiant woodstove to replace the Heatilator.

Vermont Castings was a relatively new company co-founded by a former town resident. Almost everyone renovating old homes installed woodburning stoves of varying brands. The largest and most expensive of the Vermont Castings line, the black cast-iron Defiant, had a second burn chamber enabling it, with the right amount and type of wood, to burn for twelve hours, after which only ash remained in the firebox. But those ashes usually were warm enough to ignite some paper and kindling for a repeat cycle.

Heating with electric baseboard was expensive, as was propane. Today a natural gas line parallels Highway 135; gas is cheaper and residents are richer. In the 1970s the propane was stored in green tanks, bleached white from the sun, in the rear of most homes in town, and they were serviced periodically by a large tanker-type truck. The tank in Kathy's back yard fueled the kitchen oven and stove and the water heater and only needed to be filled twice a year.

"A leaking gas tank" was then a common call to the Fire Department. The firemen hosed down the "yard bomb," which had expanded in the heat and forced the overflow of propane out of the pressure relief valve. On occasion the gas leaked from a pipe leading into the house, and the structure exploded.

Wood seemed like a safe, back-to-the-earth kind of heat for the newly arrived hippies of the 1970s and my "earth mother" sister. And aside from the gasoline for the truck and chainsaw, and one's labor, it was a cheap alternative. You were warmed three times heating with wood: first when you cut it, second when you split it, and third when you finally lit the fire. The added benefit was the lack of monthly heating bills.

Kathy had made some other improvements to the house. But when she tried to talk me into buying it that night over dinner in 1979, the Defiant was still going strong.

"Kathy, I can't afford to buy it."

"But you need a house. You can't rent forever. And I'll loan you the money. You can pay me instead of the bank. All you need to do is borrow the down payment."

"Yes, but . . ."

"No 'yes buts,'" she retorted. Then she upped the ante. "Hank will build you a darkroom next to the pot shop, and a woodshed out back. You can pay materials only."

"I don't know about the woodstove." From my seat at the kitchen table, I could see it, but I was having difficulty dealing with the idea of using it. Was it just my imagination, or was the front door of the Defiant grinning at me? Something about the shape . . . Kathy interrupted my musings.

"It's easy. I'll give you a lesson. And don't you just love the feeling of the heat?"

I had to admit her house was usually warm when I dropped by. She saw the doubt on my face and sweetened the pie some more. "And we'll move you in using the horse trailer. Won't take any time at all."

We wrote the details on a scrap of paper and took it to an attorney the next day before I could change my mind.

By then it was early November and cold enough to turn on the heat. And I don't mean turn up the thermostat. The Defiant was the one and only source of heat in the whole nine-hundred-square-foot house.

The closest I'd ever come to building a fire was watching our Dad do it on camping trips. Kathy spent a couple of hours teaching me the ropes—crumpling newspaper, stacking kindling like a little tipi so the flame would draw, stoking the Defiant, banking the fire, and how to keep it going all day and all night without burning down the house. This knowledge was critical, as the lady across the street had already destroyed her house by throwing kerosene into the woodstove before lighting it. Since Kathy was carrying the financing on my debt, it was vital that her/my house remain standing so she could collect her $204.97 per month for the next thirty years.

Once I had figured out the damper and to leave the (grinning?) door open a couple of inches at first to help the smoke draw, she showed me how to shovel the ashes into a bucket and "never, never put the bucket into the bathroom to warm it up! Always set it outside to cool before emptying it!" Ah ha, now I knew the source of the round scorch mark on the bathroom linoleum. But I wisely kept my mouth shut.

Next she demonstrated how to swing a maul to split the rounds of wood that Hank had already stacked in the new woodshed. I'd never seen a maul before—heck, I'd never heard of the word. It's like an axe, only heavier, with a longer handle and only one cutting edge.

"Now watch! You bring it up over your head and let the weight of the head carry it into the round of wood," Kathy instructed. I picked it up. And dropped it back down, then bent

Our house at 512 Sopris.

over to look at it more closely. It was a twelve-pound maul according to the imprint on the metal head. What if I swung it over my head and lost my grip?

"So, how much would it cost for me to buy wood already split?" I asked, casually leaning on the maul handle.

"A hundred dollars a cord. And you need at least five cords. Which reminds me, we need to order you a cord of apple wood or oak from Hotchkiss. You add it to the fire to keep it going through the night. But you don't have to split it. Now pay attention here! I have pots to glaze and I'm meeting Hank in two hours."

Always no nonsense, that's my sister.

My brother-in-law was more of a dreamer. Why else would he have cut three-foot diameter rounds of wood and stacked them in a shed eighty feet from the house? Since I worked all week, my only chance to get the wood rounds close to the house to split was at night or during my days off. After shoveling a fifty-foot-long path to the shed, then wrestling the heavy rounds back up the path, I found myself longing for a more conventional form of heat.

But that was just the beginning. I swung that maul for all I was worth. Often it took twenty hits before the round would split open with a "crack!" Once it was in about six pieces, I stacked the wood in the mudroom and in a pile next to the back door.

Sometimes when I arrived home to a cold house, the Defiant resisted my amateurish attempts to fire up its belly, but it wasn't totally at fault. The kindling wouldn't catch because I hadn't crumpled enough paper. Other times I added apple wood too soon before the pine

*Oak is even heavier than apple, which is heavier than pine, as I was soon to discover
when this load had to be stacked in the woodpile.*

was burning hot enough, and then the fire smoldered. If I was home most of the day stoking
the fire, the living room was so toasty I could almost wear shorts, but the bathroom was
barely up to sixty-five degrees—on a warm day. The rising heat warmed the upstairs bedroom by nightfall. But the heat was also rising right on through the uninsulated roof. Often
I questioned my sanity buying a house without piped-in heat. I kept reminding myself that I
wasn't paying out a fortune to the electric or propane company, and that helped—a little.

During the first winter when an early snowstorm dropped a foot a day, I was shoveling
the long path, shoveling out the windows, shoveling out the car, and shoveling out under
the eaves of the roof so the snow off the roof would have a place to slide. My sister came
over for a visit, and she shoveled, too. We eyed the woodshed. It didn't have much of a roof
pitch. I called Hank long distance.

"We've gotten about five feet in the past ten days. Do you think I ought to shovel the
roof of the shed?" I asked.

"Oh, no," came his confident reply. "It'll be just fine."

Kathy and I took a closer look. The rafters were bending oh-so-slightly. "Tomorrow," we
said.

The next morning I parted my bedroom window curtains. "Damn it, we should have
done it yesterday!"

Throughout the rest of the winter, I trudged the path each week to the wreck of a collapsed woodshed. The fallen snow had begun to ice up, and the freeze/thaw action froze the

The house next door belonging to Mrs. Opal Hooper in 1979.
Vacant all winter, it became pillowed with snow.

wood rounds together. Crouching under what remained of the broken roof, I pried each hunk of wood loose with the shovel and pushed it up the path.

The following summer I got out a crowbar and bribed a boyfriend with promises of dinner to help me rip it all apart and take it to the dump, rueing the day I'd paid Hank to build it. As the years went by, though, I slowly forgave him for his misjudgment. He and Kathy divorced, and I finally mastered the art of heating with wood, after replacing the fiasco of a woodshed with a woodpile outside the back door.

Throughout my thirties and early forties, I depended on the Defiant and my own muscles and brains for heat, adding push-ups to my exercise regimen to strengthen my arms and back. Steady boyfriends were intermittent, and they had their own wood to haul and split. Back then, you weren't a man unless you knew how to wield a chainsaw. Moreover, the local status symbol was not the kind of car you drove, since almost everyone drove an old pick-up truck, but the brand name of your chainsaw.

So I did it all myself every fall after I paid for the rounds of wood to be delivered. Which is not to say that friends and neighbors didn't help out occasionally. The guy who fixed my broken maul handle took a few swings on a round to make sure his repair would hold. My neighbor across the street, Lyle McNeill, born and raised here, loaned me a wedge once to

    HOT AND COLD—HEATING WITH WOOD

free my maul, which I'd stuck in a crack like King Arthur's sword. Too old and wise to chop wood, he just sat and watched for a while.

At first I was fussy about the wood chips on the lawn, fearing they would damage the grass. I soon realized the winter's snows covered the whole mess and that each spring after I raked the scraps away, the lawn grew back green as ever. If ever I was tempted to stack the wood elsewhere I thought back to the dreadful first year of rolling the rounds up the snowy path and quickly came to my senses. By the time I was finished splitting and stacking, the woodpile measured fifteen feet long by ten feet wide by as high as I could reach. With a friend's help, I covered it with a huge sheet of plastic, weighed down with chunks of wood.

In addition to splitting the wood, I made an appointment with the chimney sweep each September to brush out the stovepipe. Neglecting that chore was risking a chimney fire; almost as many houses in town burned from chimney fires as blew up from gas leaks.

Chimney fires are usually caused by a build-up of creosote, a by-product of the burning wood, or rather, smoldering wood. That's why it was important to get the fire roaring before shutting down the damper. If creosote builds up inside your stovepipe because you were too cheap to call the chimney sweep, the roaring flame could catch the creosote on fire and you'd be getting a visit from the Fire Department to hose down your roof.

The newer type of double-walled stovepipe like I had reduced the number of chimney fires, but hey, we were playing with fire here and you could never be too safe. My own accidental scorch marks, from sparks and logs that had fallen out, marred the oak floor next to the hearth.

A GIGANTIC WOODPILE IS WORTHLESS if you can't get to it. After a big snowstorm I prioritized my shoveling—first the path to the woodpile, then the top of the woodpile, gently—any large rips in the plastic would cause the melting snow to freeze the wood together. Next came the darkroom path, the car, and, depending on the magnitude of the storm and depth of snow, the house windows and roof eaves.

The below-freezing temperatures that usually arrive after a snowstorm are a big problem regardless of your heat source, although more so with a wood-burning stove. It wasn't my imagination that the heat took forever to migrate into rooms too far removed from the stove—places that invariably housed running water. Frozen pipes were not uncommon. I have a friend whose pipes froze thirty-two times in one winter, often cracking or breaking.

"The pipes always rupture at the lowest point, and as the water continues to drip, the pipe won't hold a solder," she explained. "Fritz [Yaklich] and Willard [Ruggera], town plumbers at the time, told me to stick bread up the broken pipe. The bread soaks up the water long enough to let the pipe dry so you can solder it. When everything is repaired and the water is running through the pipe again, the bread dissolves."

My crawl spaces were fairly well insulated compared to other old houses. I could usually thaw the pipes in the darkroom in a couple of days' time, wielding the hair dryer and keeping a naked light bulb on around the clock. The toilet froze in the house only a few times, and for that I hired the big guns—my friendly but expensive plumber.

More than once, though, I wistfully eyed Lyle and Mildred McNeill's home across the street, with its gas forced-air furnace. For an old-timer, Lyle was pretty progressive. Most of the old homes in town belonging to long-time residents were heated with coal. Each fall, the O.C. Company coal truck from Ohio Creek delivered to sheds in the rear of the houses, or occasionally to the basements. At the Wooden Nickel, chunks of coal slid down a chute through a basement window facing Elk Avenue. On cold mornings, a large, grey cloud of coal and wood smoke hung in the air, floating slowly down valley: the distinctive smell of winter tickling your nostrils or causing you to cough.

In 1986 the town council decided that the smog was not attractive to tourists or residents and unhealthy to breathe as well. It decreed that all woodstoves would meet a predetermined clean-air standard; either you upgraded to an emissions-free woodstove or switched to gas or electric heat. They gave everyone three years to phase out the old and bring in the new.

The town gave an informal exemption to old-timers who heated primarily with coal. Once their houses were sold or remodeled, however, the new owners would be required to convert. The ornately decorated, taller than me, nickel-plated, coal-fired potbelly stove heated the Conoco until the day Tony Mihelich died in 1996.

Former town manager Bill Crank said, "We got a report showing that coal was slightly cleaner burning, except it did have carbon monoxide particulates. So we never pressed anyone. Most people converted voluntarily."

I had my wooden "cross" to bear; others lugged their heavy, dusty coal buckets. We had a lot in common. Even though I had tamed the Defiant, I chose electric baseboard over a new woodstove and had it installed the winter before I met my husband-to-be. Just my luck, I finally had a splitting and stacking partner—about ten years too late. Greg and I sold the Defiant to a friend down valley to heat his woodworking shop. He loves it.

The town did the right thing. No longer was the morning air choked with inversion haze. No longer were my fall weekends spent getting in the wood. No longer did I have to sweep the wood chips from the living room floor next to the stove. But oh how I missed backing my butt up to that Defiant, basking in its cozy warmth.

Occasionally I see a twenty-something-year-old girl swinging a maul surrounded by a pile of split logs and more logs to split, and I am tempted to ask her for a swing—just to hear that sweet-sounding crack of success.

CHAPTER 9

Lyle's Freezer

My neighbor Lyle McNeill in 1980.

L YLE M c N EILL AND HIS WIFE, Mildred, were my across-the-street neighbors. Because of their independence and our mutual respect for each other's privacy, coupled with my shyness, our friendship was slow to grow. We didn't seek out each other's company. No dinner invitations or afternoon coffee. It was more along the lines of . . .

"Say, I'm going to be out of town for a week. Just wanted to let you know."

"Sure. I'll be glad to keep my eye on your place," he'd reply casually.

Then it progressed to . . .

"Say, I'll be visiting my folks from May 15 to the 30th. My sister is the only one you might see going in and out."

"Well, no problem. We'll be right here," he'd reply.

After I'd been living there for about eight years, I might drop by at lunchtime and grab a couple of his Fig Newtons while Lyle ate and Mildred and I talked about flower gardens.

But first we teased each other. "Lyle, have you got your hearing aid in? I need to ask you something." He would grin and pull it out from the pocket of his overalls and stick it in so he could hear me. "And sure, have a Fig Newton," he'd say.

The friendship was cemented not so much with talk as with deeds, mostly his.

When I built my darkroom in the shed behind the house, I needed to find the water line. The plumbers and I wandered around scratching our heads. Lyle ambled over, as he often did when I was outside splitting wood, shoveling snow, or otherwise messing around in the yard. I can't remember his ever knocking at the door. That's what his kitchen window was for.

"Lyle, you've put in every water line in this town. Surely you know where this one is."

"Well, let's go see what I've got."

He walked back across the street, and I tagged along. From a shelf in his garage crammed with tools and construction equipment, Lyle pulled out two long copper rods, bent the ends with a pair of pliers, and strolled back across to my lawn with them.

Lyle McNeill was a water dowser.

It might not seem much of an accomplishment to some, but when you're seeking an obscure water line in the confusion of Crested Butte's underground pipes, it's a gift.

Owner of Mac's Backhoe Service, a heavy equipment company, Lyle personally laid almost every water pipe in town. If he couldn't find it either through dowsing with his copper wands or from memory, it probably didn't exist. In this case, it existed, although it wound a circuitous underground path from the alley to the house.

After he found the line, he challenged me to do the same with my eyes closed. And sure enough as I intersected the pipe buried deep under the grass, those copper rods quivered in my hands and crossed themselves.

The contents of his garage pulled me out of a jam more than once. Over the years, I borrowed a battery charger, wire brush, crowbar, and a wedge to pry open the round of wood in which I had jammed my maul. Every time I knocked on their back door asking for help, Lyle delighted in opening the door of an old freezer in which he had stored the contents of three or four normal-sized tool chests. Everything was neatly laid out on the freezer shelves and easy to get to. Lyle's garage was a mini-hardware store. After twelve years in the construction business and twenty-seven years as the Gunnison County road foreman, Lyle had collected every nut, bolt, screwdriver, wrench, and tool known to man. There was barely enough room for their car and Lyle's precious snowblower. His pick-up truck sat outside in the driveway.

Lyle's brain was as full of historical anecdotes as his garage was full of tools.

He told me how he helped to build the Company Store, and that my house had been a hay barn on the hill above town known as Chocolate Peak. Later it was purchased by his dear cousin Alvie "Budgie" Bottenfield. Lyle himself had owned the deed for a while.

Before his eye surgery Lyle had regularly plowed my driveway in the winter with his backhoe. He wouldn't take any money, just a thank you and an occasional plate of home-baked cookies or banana bread. Mildred, of course, was a far better baker than I. But he never turned down my offerings. I think he had a surrogate father-daughter relationship with many single ladies in town. His own three daughters at the time were scattered across the country. In addition to helping me out, he plowed Mildred's mother Jessie Mae Richardson's driveway on the corner of Elk Avenue and Fourth Street. A shed and garage in the rear were sided with license plates that her husband, Ben, had tacked up over the years. Today the "License Plate House" has been renovated into a rental. The shed houses a coffee shop.

Mrs. Richardson's license plate garage and shed in 1977 before their remodel.

As one of his mayoral responsibilities, optional, of course, Lyle attached the street signs to posts at intersections, using his old Jeep as a ladder. Before signs were erected, Elk Avenue was, and still is occasionally, referred to as "Main Street."

Following his operation he sold his heavy equipment and mourned the partial loss of his eyesight to macular degeneration and the onset of old age. Then Lyle discovered snowblowers, trading up for a larger, more efficient model every couple of winters. One morning after a heavy snow, when he had finished snowblowing his own yard, I caught him pushing it down our street, clearing snow out of the gutter. "Hey, Lyle," I said half-jokingly, "if you're that bored, why not push that thing through my driveway?" And by the time I returned home from work at lunchtime, he had neatly plowed the whole driveway around my car.

I called to thank him right away. "Lyle, you saved my life and saved me about twenty dollars."

"I'm sorry I didn't make it all the way down the path to your back shed, but Mildred was calling me for lunch," he apologized.

He cleared my driveway several times afterward, and I'd call my regular driveway plow contractor to explain the situation. He was always very understanding—no way Lyle's snowblower would put him out of business.

I suspect that watching me struggle to split my winter's wood was one of Lyle's greatest sources of amusement. It had been a long time since he'd burned wood for heat. But he never lost his fondness for cutting wood. Lyle regularly got truckloads of wood from Rozman's sawmill at the upper end of Elk Avenue. The slabs, sliced from the outsides of huge logs felled up on Kebler Pass, would be considered scrap at any other sawmill. But Crested Butte natives never waste anything.

Dressed in his usual uniform of denim bib overalls, Lyle spent the day cutting them into sixteen-inch pieces, then delivering a truckload to each of the women in the neighborhood—those with no man, no roommate, or no money. I took a vacation one snowy spring and returned to find a pile of the kindling next to my house.

Even after I converted to electric heat, Lyle still asked me each fall if I wanted any wood. When I demurred, he'd tell me he had to cut some for his daughters Connie and Shari, who had moved to Gunnison. Did I have any friends who wanted some?

Next to his wife, daughters, and garage, the Senior Citizens Center, which he founded, was Lyle's pride and joy. Every day he fired up his truck and drove the three blocks uptown to unlock the door and sit inside or out, depending on the weather, to chat with whomever dropped by.

He let me hang my old-timer photos there, and before his eyesight got worse, loved nothing better than to move them around, climbing a stepladder, hammering nails, and grouping them by family. He accidentally broke the glass on a photo of a woman who had moved away. Apologizing, he gave it to me and casually remarked, "Never did like that woman." I didn't replace the glass, knowing Lyle probably wouldn't hang it anyway.

Before each Memorial Day parade, Mildred and Lyle came up to the center early. She made coffee. He straightened up the tables and chairs and later enjoyed catching up with all the former residents who returned for the celebration.

Lyle's last Memorial Day was in May 1991. He had suffered a series of small strokes, was undergoing therapy, and tired easily. But he insisted that Mildred bring him up to the cen-

Jessie Richardson and her great-granddaughter Melina Cobai in 1975.

Joe Rozman cuts slabs off a big log at his sawmill in 1973.

ter. After making the painful steps in his walker from the curb through the door, Lyle was enthroned on a folding chair by the entrance, where old friends hugged him, grasped his hand, and spoke a few words. The strokes had robbed him of the ability to put in words how happy he was to be among friends. But you could see it in his eyes.

Lyle's strokes had been preceded by a fall earlier the previous winter on the ice in front of the Company Store. He had regularly walked uptown late in the afternoon or after dinner to have a beer at the Talk of the Town with his friends Joe Sedmak and Botsie Spritzer. One such walk resulted in the cracked pelvis that kept him homebound using a walker. On warmer days, he bundled up and ventured out onto his front porch to fall asleep in the sun.

Once when I came over and woke him up for a talk, he got teary-eyed telling me how much Mildred meant to him—how he couldn't have made it without her. Married in Gunnison on June 30, 1934, Lyle and Mildred had fifty years of good times and bad. We joked about how Mildred was always nagging at him to walk farther to keep strong. He walked as far as the bars between Second and Third Streets. Mildred went all the way to First Street. I often wish I'd asked him more about the early days and his childhood. I did learn that his mother's name was Henrietta and that she had been born in Illinois in 1886. She met her husband, Thomas, in Lafayette, Colorado, and moved to Crested Butte in 1911. Lyle was born April 22, 1912, on a ranch now occupied by the Crested Butte Community School at the edge of town.

*Camera-shy Mildred McNeill only consented to be photographed in 1979 upon Lyle's insistence.
He was hanging all my old-timer photos in the Senior Citizens Center and wanted hers to be included.
I dropped by their house when she was baking biscuits for a local restaurant. After two frames, she said,
"That's enough now." I was lucky to talk her into letting me shoot another six frames.*

Two days before the final x-ray that would show his pelvis completely healed, I was shoveling five inches of new snow. Hearing the noise of an engine in our normally quiet neighborhood, I looked across the street to see that Lyle had left his walker at the back door and was running the snowblower around his truck. I ran over like an overprotective mother. He grinned like a schoolboy caught playing hooky, waved off my concern, and revved the blower up another notch. Mildred was wringing her hands and shaking her head in the kitchen.

"I can't do anything with him. He just insisted on blowing that snow. I told him Steve [Baker] would plow it later. But he wouldn't hear of it."

Just like Lyle. Never a man to be indebted to anyone. Never a man to remain inactive. After twenty years on the Crested Butte Town Council, six years as mayor, thirty-four years as a member of the Gunnison County Electric Association board of directors (ten as president), a couple of stints on the school and hospital boards, and 1978 King of Flauschink, the feisty redhead (his hair had long ago turned snow white) wasn't about to sit on his butt now. He loved machinery, his backhoe, a good polka party, and elk hunting.

The strokes that came after his pelvis mended eventually landed him in the hospital and the Gunnison Health Care Center for rehabilitation. "I'm sure Lyle just needs a couple of months of therapy to recover," Mildred told me.

As his health worsened, however, they realized a move to Gunnison with its milder climate and proximity to doctors and the hospital would be necessary.

After their new Gunnison home was finished, their daughters moved them in one spring while I was on vacation. Noticing the absence of curtains on the windows when I returned, I walked over and peeked in the garage window. Empty! Those wonderful tools and shelves of odds and ends, even the freezer—all gone. I was crushed. I never had a chance to say farewell.

Eventually Lyle gave up. He was a man full of energy trapped in a body that just wouldn't say yes anymore. He tried to fight the wheelchair and the bed that they had to strap him into for his own safety.

He lost his battle on October 1, 1992. He was eighty.

Crested Butte lost, too. We lost a man full of knowledge, history, skill, and kindness.

And I lost my across-the-street neighbor, who, over the years, became so much more than just a neighbor.

CHAPTER 10

Flauschink Is Comink!

My photo of Botsie Spritzer playing the accordion as king of the 1982 Flauschink celebration was made into a poster, and Botsie was thrilled to pose with it the following year.

Halfway through the ski season of 1969 a trio of locals sat around the Grubstake Bar one evening and decided that Crested Butte needed its very own spring bash to send winter on its way. "Not with a whimper, but a bang," as editor George Sibley wrote in the next issue of the *Crested Butte Chronicle*. George's imaginative partners were Chuck Wirtz, local bon vivant and bartender; and Art Norris, college professor and wit. But Flauschink was mostly George's baby. As he put it: "It was a slow news week, so we invented a celebration."

George wrote about observing an old man who mysteriously appeared on a local bar stool. He chugged a shot of slivovitz from his rubber galosh, threw back his head, and growled "Flauschink!" before disappearing into the stormy night. An old-timer sitting nearby informed George that the stranger was an "Ugra Sorbian" and that "Flauschink" was a toast the Ugra Sorbians used to express their joy for the end of winter and the coming of spring.

Gene Martin, local loquacious entrepreneur, called George to shoot a photo for the next issue of the *Chronicle* of an ancient, carved wooden mask he claimed to have dug up in the back yard of his gift shop on Elk Avenue. It had been verified by one Allen Smedhurst, archaeologist, as an authentic Ugra-Sorbian relic, thus confirming the mysterious stranger's heritage and his unusual toast.

"Flauschink" sounded like a pretty good name to George, Chuck, and Art for the festival they had in mind, which would mirror the Ugra Sorbians' feelings about winter's end. Luckily, or maybe just accidentally, instead of a trite title like "Springfest," we celebrate "Flauschink" the weekend the ski area closes.

Those stories and photos provided George with news for about three issues, which, back in those days, was quite a feat. The town council met only once a month, there was no board of zoning, and the most exciting news might have been fifteen inches of new snow.

Okay, that's how I remember it. And since it was all a concoction anyway (although George continues to swear just the opposite), I suppose the "facts" surrounding Flauschink's birth will remain a bit foggy. Suffice it to say it was the first of many festivals, winter or summer, dreamed up by Crested Butte's newcomers. It wasn't for tourists. It was for locals. No longer would ski season wind down like a tired, battery-powered toy with many young folks slinking off to Mexico to escape the impending mud season. Instead we planned for— indeed, longed for—that final weekend. We started celebrating on Friday, and really whooped it up on Saturday and Sunday. Monday morning, nursing hangovers and sunburns, everyone who could afford it and many who couldn't threw the skis in the shed and high-tailed it south.

That first Flauschink began with a torchlight parade down the ski slopes. Ski school and ski patrol members took the last ride up at four p.m. and enjoyed a private celebration in the upper patrol shack, fueled by flasks smuggled in jacket pockets. The drink of choice was hot chocolate liberally spiked with peppermint schnapps. When darkness fell, they skied from the top of the gondola lift to the base area, carrying lighted torches instead of ski poles. As they began their serpentine run, one behind the other, a flaming peace symbol was outlined on the face of the International ski run. An unplanned event, chief suspects were the ski patrol members since they were the only ones having access to the torches. At the bottom everyone sizzled their flames into the snow and surveyed the damage to ski jackets, pants, and gloves from the sparks.

Later in the evening Cathy Wertz and Crested Butte native Whitey Sporcich were crowned the king and queen during the polka party at Frank and Gal's Bar downtown. Homemade crowns of silver spray-painted cardboard, tastefully lined with colorful feathers, were placed on the heads of the slightly embarrassed duo. A dark-haired young dynamo from Denver, Cindy Quint, played the accordion while we polka-danced across the oiled wooden floor. (In later years Botsie Spritzer, George's sports editor, would entertain on his accordion, and the crowns, while still homemade, became more elaborate and zany.) George showed up with an old rubber boot similar to the one from which the Ugra Sorbian gentleman had swigged his slivovitz. It was a fuzzy Friday evening, the memory of which is captured in my equally fuzzy photos (I still hadn't bought a flash attachment) of George chugging beer from the boot.

The next day the T-bar slope was the Flauschink playground—three-legged ski races, inner-tube races, a beer slalom, ski school versus ski patrol slalom race, and, most exciting of all, the gelandesprung. Different than the free-heel ski jumping you see at the Olympics, gelande contestants wearing standard alpine fixed-heel bindings were judged on the outrageous tricks they performed in the air. The best alpine jumpers in the county tried to outdo each other with daffys, spread eagles, back scratchers, somersaults, and the like—all of them on long skis of about 220 centimeters, not the shorties of 140 or so today. The more tricks you could do before landing, the higher the score. Another gelande was for distance jumping only. By 1974, local merchants had begun to put up cash prizes.

Since it was Easter weekend, we held an outdoor church service in Paradise Bowl. Their majesties Cathy and Whitey reigned over it all, ferried to and fro in a snowcat, containing, of course, liquid refreshment and a retinue of Flauschink committee members, girlfriends, husbands, wives, and hangers on.

The enthusiasm carried over into the second year as George, Chuck, and Art added a Grand Parade on Saturday night, complete with a hay wagon hauling the royalty—Barbara Sibley and Rudy Sedmak. Their "chariot" quickly developed a flat tire. Behind came a ragtag group of merrymakers brandishing rag and kerosene stake torches, and another wagon with the Western State College band. A ski instructor blew a bugle to herald the arrival of the royalty at each bar.

Barbara and Rudy were in for a surprise when they walked into the Tailings Bar in the basement of the Company Store. The low ceiling was gaily festooned with streamers of toilet paper. At one end of the room were their thrones, looking as if they came straight out of

 FLAUSCHINK IS COMINK!

Garth Hammond's gelande jump in 1970 was a total disaster,
and he knew it coming down.

someone's washroom, if you get my drift. Their scepters—toilet bowl plungers. And that's how Flauschink ("flushing" the season out, of course, according to the intent of the founders) acquired its bathroom theme.

The design of the colorful Flauschink buttons, the sale of which supported the festival, was decidedly in that direction in 1974, 1978, and through most of the 1980s. The different years depicted outhouses, toilet paper rolls, plungers, and a toilet being flushed by a mischievous-looking elf. From that second year on, the bravest of the royalty and committee drank out of the plunger-scepters (bought new for the occasion each year, we were told). After a few hits of champagne, beer, or poison of your choice, you hardly noticed the rubber taste. In 1989, honoring the 20th anniversary of the old man drinking from the boot in the bar, the button featured a boot brimming with beer foam.

The gelande was full of surprises in 1970, the biggest being a jump by a ski instructor who attempted nobody knows what—a somersault, we think—and almost landed on his head. I captured him upside-down, arms and legs flailing, in a photo that became the 1971 Flauschink poster. Usually held under the gondola lift line at Tower Seven, the gelande could be seen from the lift (its colorful three-person cars since replaced by the Silver Queen high-speed quad chair) and from the run-out near the T-bar road. Spectators climbed trees and pressed against snow fences to get a glimpse of the action.

The king and queen of Flauschink have always been chosen in absolute secrecy and, without question, undemocratically by the committee members. The wittiest member of the committee usually creates a funny poem detailing personality quirks or accomplishments. The final line names the new king or queen. George, Chuck, and Art had wit and puns coming out their ears. Since they felt it important that a local celebration include all locals, the royalty reflected that. The trend soon became obvious—a newcomer woman, usually young, and an old-timer man. In 1971 I figured my time had come; it looked like they were running out of newcomer ladies, and of all the young newcomers, I'd been here the longest. Unlike some mountain women, I'll admit I would have loved to be a queen—of something, though I'd rather have died than tell anyone. But in a reversal of tradition that year, the committee chose a young, old-timer female and a "new-timer" male.

I settled for shared fame by loaning my photos to graphic artist Susan Anderton, who used them as the basis for her silk-screened posters advertising Flauschink throughout the 1970s and into the '80s. It was an incentive each year to come up with unusual shots, which Susan would critically scan with her artist's eye before making her choice. She transformed my black-and-white photographs into vivid color prints, many of which have become collectors' items, particularly the early ones. All limited-edition runs, they were offered for sale in her gallery. Once her supply was gone, she never reprinted them.

By 1972 George had retired as editor of the *Chronicle* and moved to Gothic with his family, and Art had relocated down valley. Chuck asked me, along with Cal Queal, public relations director at the ski area, to join him on the committee. Cal became the parade marshal and ski area liaison, while George, who skied down from Gothic for the day, shared announcing duties with Chuck at the Coronation Ball and on the T-bar. My contribution as ed-

Susan Anderton and Chuck Wirtz, their majesties in 1979.

itor of the *Crested Butte Pilot* was multifold. I distributed buttons, picking up money when I took the newspapers around town to bars and shops each Friday. I was generally the "rah rah" woman hyping the event in the *Pilot* for at least three weeks before. Many news stories bore the headline "Flauschink Is Comink!" And if the advertising could support it, I printed a full page of photos afterwards.

For some long-forgotten reason, we moved the Flauschink parade to Saturday at eleven a.m. One April morning the temperature never got above twenty-five degrees *below zero.* Shivering in the open car during the parade, the king let forth with a royal edict:

"I proclaim I am freezing my ass and we're going to the Wooden Nickel for a shot of whiskey."

The parade detoured, or rather flat stopped, before its official ending at Second Street so His Majesty, Fred Drury, could go inside and warm up. Meeting at a local bar following the parade became a tradition that has extended to the July Fourth parade as well.

Once installed on the committee, I had to give up my dream of queen for a weekend. Instead I helped to pen the poems, most of which are lost to posterity; a few were published in the newspaper. All three of us assisted in making sure that the chosen ones showed up at the crowning. And of course we led the general partying and helped to organize the events.

One year a lack of snow placed the beer slalom on Warming House Hill, where a snowball fight broke out around the water gate, an obstacle created by the spontaneous discovery of water under the slushy snow. As each skier raced down the hill and tried to jump over the pond, many ended up in the drink, creating quite a splash, literally and figuratively.

In subsequent years the infamous Beer Slalom, loosely organized by Western State College's Luftseben (a drinking club is the best way to describe it), morphed into a tamer Saloon Slalom for bartenders, complete with gates where the racer had to balance a tray of glasses. We added a hot dog race for show-offs on the upper runs of the mountain. A couple of characters paddling down the Jokerville run in a rubber raft were the hit of the event.

A matched pair of daredevils won the gelande in 1972. One did a backflip while his partner flipped frontward simultaneously. And for those getting a head start on spring, a motorcycle race was held to see who could get the farthest up Warming House Hill. For the really crazy, a ski-jouring contest—skiers pulled by snowmobile steeplechase—took place near a condo complex. A few years later we added a tug of war on skis and a freestyle ski event.

Thanks to a wet T-shirt contest that year at a local bar—not Flauschink-sponsored, but exciting just the same—we got national press coverage, or rather the winner of the contest did. No matter. Flauschink was on its way to being a tourist event by 1973. But that was about the time the gelande lost its craziness. "Inverted" maneuvers were outlawed because of accidents at other ski areas resulting in paralysis to a couple of competitors. In other words, no more flips. The gelande was judged on distance only

I retired from the committee in the late 1970s after selling the *Crested Butte Pilot.* I like to think that Flauschink peaked during my time. Later I could see it becoming a formula event, and each year I shot fewer and fewer photographs. I even had to miss a Flauschink Ball during the '80s—my first ever—when I had pneumonia and the doctor threatened me with a hospital stay. I lay feverish in bed, rationalizing that I could shoot a photo of the royalty for the *Mountain Sun* newspaper, my employer at the time, the following morning during the parade. As the polka party roared on at Rozman's Motor Inn behind my house, I was too sick to care. Many years later a committee member let slip that it was to have been my

     FLAUSCHINK IS COMINK!

We often met at Matt and Mary Volk's house before the Flauschink parade.
In 1988, Mary sports her Flauschink button-decorated hat.

Bea and Art Norris enjoy a Flauschink polka dance in 1989.

night for crowning. No one had bothered to make sure I was coming. After all, they knew I'd be there to take pictures for the paper. Wasn't I always?

Today you'll see a wagon full of "Has Beens"—former royalty—riding in the Flauschink parade, carousing and toasting each other and the day with champagne and beer. I occasionally jump on to join my friends, many of whom don't even realize I've never been crowned. Not a "Has Been" exactly but an "Almost Been." And I suppose that'll have to do.

CHAPTER 11

Mushroom Fever

Tom Snellar in 1979 with his trophy puffball mushroom.
"I'm going to cut it up and fry it like steak," he said.

"PUT ON YOUR HIKING BOOTS and grab a couple of garbage bags. The Sporciches are taking us mushrooming," announced my mother.

Wait a minute. I had always picked the mushrooms out of her casseroles, and now I was expected to pick them out of the earth? However, it was a clear summer morning in the late 1960s, and after days of rain, I was happy to get out of the house. Only years later would I understand what a compliment it was to be invited.

We drove toward Kebler Pass and then up a series of switchbacks, for what seemed like hours, before stopping at the highest one. Everyone piled out, garbage bags in hand. Our next-door neighbors showed us our quarry: a yellow mushroom with irregularly patterned gills and a dry, firm cap. Returning home later with our treasure of wild golden chanterelles, we cleaned them all weekend on our adjoining back porches.

My distaste for mushrooms not withstanding, after that adventure I changed my tune. If I was going to do all that work, I might as well at least *taste* the fruits of my labor. My gourmet cook of a mother gently sautéed them in butter and added a dash of salt. The yellow slowly turned to brown as the moisture cooked out. Next she portioned them into muffin tins and put them in the freezer for a few hours, popped out the frozen "muffins," and wrapped them before returning them to the freezer. Then she could grab a few whenever she needed them.

I grew to love their nutty, distinctive flavor with steak or hamburger, in omelets, or on a thick slice of homemade bread. Even more than the taste, I was hooked on the search itself.

Each summer since then, my family looked to the rains as a portent of good mushroom hunting. As novices, we just tramped out anywhere into the woods on public land, or what we thought was public land, keeping our noses to the ground. Certain spots could be depended upon to yield year after year. Finding new patches was the challenge. After a time, we came to recognize a type of micro-ecosystem: the edge of the pine trees, the pitch of the slope, the way the sun slants on an open patch of ground, and the vegetation, whose name I can't tell you but whose leaves I recognize in an instant. The chanterelles hide anywhere— under rocks, at the entrance to small rodent holes, within tall grass, and at the edge of streams or small ponds.

It's an unwritten rule of hunting not to cut every mushroom in the patch. Leave the little ones so when you return after the next rain, they'll be grown up and you'll spot the patch from a distance. And bypass the too-large ones that are overripe. They'll spread the spores. Or so I was told by my friend and mycology expert, Cathy Cripps, who knew the scientific ins and outs of the mushroom and the Latin names of each species.

"The more I learn about them, the less I eat them," she said with a botanist's knowing smile.

Seeking out the odd varieties, with a straw basket over her arm and a tan hat protecting her from the sun, she wrapped colorful specimens in wax paper and later peered at them under her microscope, taking notes. Whenever I found a weird mushroom, I'd save it for her to inspect. We both knew the amanita, which is considered psychedelic but could also make you sick as a dog. Shiny red-orange with white spots, it is officially classified as poisonous and is reputed to be so dangerous that you didn't even want it in your bucket contaminating your precious chanterelles.

Cathy and I often hunted together once she knew I could keep my mouth shut and not reveal the location of her prized mushroom patches. Cathy chose the destination, I provided four-wheel-drive transportation, and she led me to the best places, but not before she swore me to secrecy. If you think I'm going to reveal where we went, forget it. She trained me well. It opened my eyes to the trust the Sporciches had placed in us when they took us up the switchbacks.

Cathy taught me how to field strip. I once compared our buckets: my mushrooms were coated with pine needles, bits of grass, dirt, and stray duff. Hers were spotless, or so it seemed. I then learned how to carefully slice the stem *above* the earth, and take time to wipe off the pine needles and grass before putting it in the bucket, making cleaning at home less of a chore.

"How do you find a good patch?" I asked her once, wanting to discover one all by myself.

"When I get close to the little devils, my nose starts to twitch."

She wasn't the only one with secrets. Old-timer Tom Snellar, who putt-putted up to his secret patches in his decrepit truck, all alone, took a few of those locations to the grave with him, including where, in 1979, he found the largest mushroom of his whole life. When he returned to town with his treasure, he looked me up to have his photograph taken holding a six-pound, white round puffball. "For proof," he explained.

Cathy and I found more than just mushrooms on our outings. Once, a melting snowbank yielded a six-pack of beer left by the previous year's elk hunters. We had a slow, giggly, tipsy ride back to town.

Invariably, when we came out of the woods and were in the car, we found it hard to get our eyes up off the ground. Even the roadsides had potential for treasure. As we drove down from our mushroom patch, Cathy scanned the embankment on the uphill side and spotted some king boletes, a spongy brown mushroom bigger than your outstretched hand, which, unless you picked it at the height of its ripeness, was apt to be wormy. I thought them too slimy and didn't care for the taste. But Cathy loved them.

"Stop the car! Let's go road hunting!"

She scrambled up the embankment and walked along the top. I had the visual advantage. She had the knife. I inched the car along, paralleling her steps twenty feet above me; I held the bucket out my window with one hand and the steering wheel with the other, spotting mushrooms below her.

"There, Cath, slightly below your left foot. It's hidden from you by that rock."

Cathy Cripps in 1983, with her own puffball, doing a Tom Snellar imitation.

"Got it!"

She carefully tossed down each large bolete into my bucket. These were for eating, not looking at under the microscope.

After Cathy moved back East to earn her master's degree in mycology in the early 1980s, I was back to solitary hunting. Strolling along, I'd bend forward slightly, knees bent, hands clasped behind my back, eyes scanning across the earth. My conscious mind stilled its chatter while my subconscious relaxed and worked out gnawing problems. I found it restful mentally, yet tiring physically—an excellent combination. Even more than the mushrooms, the reward was an intangible, spiritual respite from noise, people, pressure, job, and day-to-day life.

When my mother visited, I had a partner once more. Every other day she'd pester me to take her out. And I'd comply after each rainstorm. So we wouldn't lose each other, we'd whistle periodically as we strayed further from the car and each other. One day our system failed us. The lure of the mushroom was too strong, and we wandered out of hearing distance from each other. Figuring she'd show up as she tired, I waited for an hour at the car, whistling, shouting, and honking the horn. I rehearsed in my mind what I would tell the search and rescue people. Judging there were two hours of sunlight left, I reluctantly headed toward town, hoping she'd dash out of the woods when she heard the engine. About a mile from where we had parked I found her on the side of the dirt road—head down, slowly walking—road hunting, of course.

"Mother, you scared the bejeesus out of me! I was on my way to get the rescue party." My fear angered me. But she was unfazed.

"I figured you had to go back to town eventually, and when I came out on the road, I didn't feel like backtracking."

I got lost myself a few times. Although I usually confined my hunting to a ten-mile radius of Crested Butte, I once took a friend's map, scrawled on a cocktail napkin, into the Taylor Park area. He spoke of wondrous acres of mushrooms poking their heads out of a carpet of pine needles.

"Stop at the little trailer by the river and visit with Opal from Oklahoma; she'll show you where to cross the river," he said.

Armed with several large garbage bags, a plastic bucket, and my backpack, which held a banana, water bottle, and Bug Off for the mosquitoes, I followed his rough map.

An older lady was relaxing in her lawn chair in front of the silver travel trailer when I arrived.

"Hi, I'm Chuck's friend from Crested Butte. Is it okay if I look for mushrooms here?"

"Sure, honey. It's Forest Service land over there, not mine. I don't get much in the way of visitors in this neck of the woods though I spend every summer here." A radiant smile lit her face.

We crossed the stream; she pointed me in the right direction and then returned to her lawn chair. I was in heaven. Chanterelles were spread out like spilled gold nuggets in front of me. I'd walk a few feet and crouch to pick the largest in a ring, then walk a few more feet

A handful of golden chanterelles.

and repeat. The canopies of the surrounding pine trees almost hid the sky. It was exactly as Chuck had described.

I filled the first garbage bag and stuffed it into my pack. The second bag grew almost too heavy to carry. So I headed back to the stream and my car, parked at Opal's trailer, to unload my precious burden. But, where was the stream?

I walked a short distance trying to hear the water. I backtracked, then started left, then right. I tried to remember where the sun was when I started. But that was three hours ago. The sun had moved. I fought down the panic. If only I had a compass. Hell, if only I'd ever learned to use a compass. In a crazy moment I considered laying out a giant, yellow SOS of mushrooms on a brown meadow of pine needles so the search planes would find me. God knows I had enough of them.

Finally, my circular walking brought me to an opening through which I could see a road. Relief flooded me. I still had the creek to cross, and as I sought the narrow, fordable place, my back ached for a chair. Then I spotted the roof of Opal's trailer.

"So, you were successful."

I answered her with a weak smile. Finally reaching her trailer door, I plopped onto the ground, too proud to admit that I had lost my way. I showed her my booty instead and offered her some.

Those bags of mushrooms had set an all-time personal record. Driving home, I saw days of cleaning stretching before me and wondered if my refrigerator had enough room to hold them all during the process. On a hunch, I stopped at the Soupçon Restaurant and peeked in the back door. The chef was prepping for dinner.

"Do you want to buy any mushrooms?"

He wiped his hands on his white apron and looked at me carefully.

"Do you know what kind you picked?"

"Of course. They are all chanterelles."

Did he think I was an idiot? Then it dawned on me he was worried about the amanitas.

He dumped part of my bag onto his table and sorted through it, culling out the best and cleanest. Field stripping had paid off.

"I'll pay you $10 a pound," he said.

Yes. I was rich!

I tried my luck at another upscale restaurant. They offered to trade my mushrooms for a dinner for two. Deal.

Two dry summers passed. The third year it rained and rained, and I returned to "Opal's patch." She was happy to see me again, remembered my car, and even recalled what we had talked about.

Shaking her head when she saw my garbage bags and bucket, she silently led me across the stream and into what had been the forest. Where the dense groves of tall trees and their pine needles had yielded up their prize, only scarred muddy earth littered with stumps and dead branches remained.

"The Forest Service sold this tract for a timber cut," she explained. "They had already logged most of the trees by the time I arrived in June."

It was my first experience with the Forest Service's Multiple Use concept of the 1970s. They managed the land for recreation, mining, timbering, fishing, and grazing; I guess mushrooming didn't rank up there with hunting and fishing. Maybe they didn't even consider it recreation. Had they been able to see into the future, they might have guarded our mushroom patch more fiercely.

IN THE EARLY 1990s a few Crested Butteans founded an annual mushroom festival where visitors and locals get together and trade recipes, learn identification procedures and mushroom cultivation, and pay for lectures on medicinal aspects. Even the restaurants get into the act and offer special dinners with wild mushroom specialties.

"Does Cathy Cripps ever come to the festival?" I asked the director. Except through mutual friends, we hadn't kept in touch. I did know that she'd married Don Bachman and had earned her mycology doctorate degree.

"No. She does technical lectures—mostly scholarly stuff—at the Telluride Mushroom Festival."

It was gratifying to learn that Cathy was one of the few of us actually making money with her college degree.

"Do you really take people out to the secret places and—?"

"No, no," the director assured me. "We have permission to hunt on private land, so we don't go to any local's hot spots."

I knew that the "hot spots" were becoming less and less of a secret as the town's population increased. But I appreciated his thoughtfulness.

And so our unorganized, spur-of-the-moment, "let's go picking this afternoon" mushroom culture has gone mainstream. Now it's about "experiential learning," according to the Crested Butte Wild Mushroom Festival brochure. I wonder if they talk about nose twitches and go road hunting?

CHAPTER 12

The Kochevar Family

*My 1968 photo of Fritz Kochevar at Frank and Gal's Bar
won a prize from the Colorado Press Association.*

In a town six blocks wide by three blocks long, where almost everyone walked everywhere, Fritz Kochevar was an anomaly. Fritz drove his gray Chevy sedan one-half block from his home at Second Street and Elk Avenue to Tony's Tavern almost every afternoon. He'd ease into a diagonal parking space on Elk Avenue—this was before the street was paved, and the sidewalks were still crumbling— slowly climb the three stairs through the door of Tony's, and nurse a few beers and maybe shoot some pool.

Then he'd slip off the stool and mosey over to Frank and Gal's to sip a few more and trade stories with his buddies. At the end of the day, he got back into the Chevy and drove the half-block up the street to his place. Where the car was parked, so was Fritz. He wasn't the only old-timer to drive to the block between Second and Third Streets, where most of the bars were located. But he had the shortest distance between his house and a bar stool.

Hunchbacked from a mine injury, Fritz smoked filter cigarettes from a white plastic holder, which I thought was pretty sophisticated for an old miner. I figured he'd roll his own. His normal attire was a dark jacket and short-brimmed newsboy cap that covered his baldness.

When I met him in 1969, he was sixty-two, young by today's standards but old for a miner. After hearing about his background I could understand why he drove that half-block for a beer.

Little by little over the years, we got to know each other; I took his picture, and he taught me how to play pool. Even after five beers, he could stand at the wrong end of the cue and tell me (or any other young girl) which way to move it. And if I carefully followed his directions, we both watched delighted as the ball rolled right into the pocket.

When he discovered I was from Arizona, he told me about his citrus trees.

"My mom just stuck a seed in a coffee can. Must have been fifty years ago. I got an orange, lemon, and grapefruit tree. Sometimes they have fruit," he said.

And one sunny day he took me to his home to show me the trees.

"I'm gonna leave this winter again, and I need you to take care of them. The orange tree died last winter while I was gone," he said, unlocking the front door.

Housed in a couple of old five-gallon metal buckets, the citrus trees fanned their branches across the width of the dirty south-facing windows, where the sun filtered onto the dusty backs of stuffed eagles, trophy animals, and a huge buffalo head hanging from the walls. The ornately carved, mirrored back bar, handcrafted by Fritz's father, Jacob, stretched the length of the room.

I'll never forget the tour that Fritz gave me; an upstairs, downstairs, and back room full of antiques, treasures, and wonderful junk—an old roulette wheel, a slot machine, and many more stuffed birds. Years later I learned that his brother Jake was the taxidermist, self-taught using a book he'd ordered from the Northwestern School of Taxidermy in Nebraska.

     THE KOCHEVAR FAMILY

That day I was struck by the sheer quantity of animals mounted on every inch of vacant wall space.

Tools, cans of nuts and bolts, and an ancient truck filled the small side shed, which Jake told me, thirty-five years later, had been their dad's workshop and blacksmith shop, where he sharpened picks used in the mines.

Fritz was the third child and the only one of his nine brothers and sisters still living in Crested Butte. He had made his home in the former saloon, which hadn't been open for business since the mines closed in 1952. His modest, personal space was dwarfed by the large, empty barroom, devoid of decoration save for the stuffed birds. A small coal stove with a pipe stretching to the high pressed tin ceiling seemed to be the only source of heat in the building. To one side of the stove were two wooden chairs drawn up to a square table. On the other side of a half-wall partition, I could see his bed.

As I wandered out the door easing from history into the present 1970s, I noticed the photo I had given him—an eight-by ten-inch black-and-white print identical to the framed one I had hung in Frank and Gal's Bar with his signature on the mat. He had tacked it up on the wall below the animal heads. Like the other old-timers, he was shy about being photographed. I glowed with pride just seeing it.

Fritz's building made an impression on other folks as well—the Walt Disney Company used it while making the film "Snowball Express" in Crested Butte in 1972. The plot was weak, but the locals were thrilled to work as extras. A snowmobile race down Elk Avenue used almost every available body in Crested Butte during the crowd scenes. The production staff dolled up Fritz's building as a gas station, bypassing the town's real gas station, Tony's Conoco. In front they put up fake pumps and a sign that read "L. L. Dingman, Auto Repairs." The ancient truck was hauled out of the side shed, and Disney added a rack with tires, plus lots of tools and junk—some of it probably belonging to Fritz, as authentic as it looked.

The following year, when asked, Fritz said he "might" attend the world premiere to be held at the Princess Theater, Crested Butte's tiny, 163-seat, one and only movie house since 1918.

All the movie hoopla was just one short chapter in Fritz's personal history. But he wasn't impressed with Hollywood, and when all the commotion died down and the truck was put away and the signs were removed, he continued with his daily routine: swapping stories and drinking beer with his fellow retired miners warming the bar stools.

What I know about him was partially gleaned from random afternoon chats. Occasionally I took notes on the back of a cocktail napkin and stuffed it in my pocket to be deciphered later. Once he had a hope that I might be his tree savior he became a bit more talkative. He enlightened me as to the purpose of the two-story outhouses behind his building, the Old Town Hall, and the Masonic Hall: "so people living upstairs didn't have to walk downstairs to go to the john."

Then he informed me, "Yugoslavian women were good at smoking and spitting tobacco. The Italian women weren't."

Fritz Kochevar's building in 1972 was used as a set for a Walt Disney movie.

"As children," Fritz continued, "we used to ski on boards and barrel staves from where the ski area is now down to the cemetery. Then we'd toboggan from the hill up Kebler Pass down to the bridge. I used to go through woodpiles to find good wood for skis—needed to be eight or nine feet long. But when I found a good piece without any knotholes in it, my dad would take it. He was a carpenter."

One afternoon Fritz and I were having a beer at Tony's when he announced, "My dad finished the diamond (patterned) floor at Frank and Gal's Bar (across the street), which was owned then by Gus Mattivi. Leonard Larsen, a Swede, started the floor, and the boards had cracks where they didn't meet evenly. So when Larsen was asked what he was going to do about the cracks, he said, 'fill 'em with sh—.'"

And he laughed at his tale. I soon learned, however, that Fritz's grandfather, Jacob Kochevar Sr., and his dad, Jacob Stefan Kochevar, were among the best carpenters in town.

Both Jacobs crafted Kochevar's Saloon from hand-hewn logs in the space of four years, beginning in 1896. Part-way through the construction, Jacob Stefan's wife died. He later met Karolina Orazem in Leadville and brought her back to Crested Butte to be his new wife. The original plans had been to make the upper story into a brothel. Legend says she put her foot down—it would be either the brothel or her. He couldn't have both. So the

     THE KOCHEVAR FAMILY

upper story remained unfinished and was used as a storage room. The saloon opened in 1900 with oilcloth on the tables and round-backed wooden chairs.

In 1916 father and son built a log structure just down the alley from the saloon. Today it's the Soupçon Restaurant, which has seen at least two additions since the 1980s.

According to my friend Trudy Yaklich, a Kochevar descendent, Jacob Kochevar Sr. arrived from Slovenia in 1883. As was the custom, he sent for his wife, Marija, and their children, Jacob Stefan among them, in 1888, after he was established in America. Trudy's grandmother Frances was the first child of Slovenian descent born in Crested Butte, in 1890.

In addition to finishing up Mattivi's floor and working with his dad on Kochevar's Saloon, the younger Jacob built the Malensek family house at the corner of First Street and Maroon Avenue in 1925. His son, my friend Fritz, born in 1906, was more of a jack-of-all-trades kind of guy and didn't follow in his father's footsteps. As a young man, he helped his brothers Rudy and Jake and their cousin John Tezak raise mink in a long shed to the west of an old boarding house on Elk Avenue, which burned in the 1970s.

Trudy remembers touring the mink farm when she was six or seven years old.

"There were cages and cages of them: tiny, little things in a long building. I suppose they sold them to a furrier in Denver for mink coats."

Legend has it that Jacob Sr. and Jacob Stefan Kochevar also built the boarding house and the Victorian-style house next door, restored by Dana Atchley in the 1970s. John Tezak Jr., another Kochevar descendent, disputes that, telling me that the boarding house was built long before his and Trudy's great-grandfather Jacob arrived in Crested Butte.

"My Uncle Rudy Kochevar told me that it was the first post office in Crested Butte," he recalled. [Rudy, Fritz's brother, ran a barbershop in the little red building on Elk Avenue that became my *Crested Butte Pilot* office.]

Rudy and his father, Jacob Stefan Kochevar, remodeled the downstairs of the boarding house by adding two rooms on its northwest corner in the early 1940s.

As for the Atchley house, John said, "My mom (Carolyn Kochevar), dad, and I moved to that house in 1934. A two-room apartment had already been added to the house. My dad installed the electrical lights, and later, he and Grandpa Jake put in a water system." Before then, John's mother hauled water from Coal Creek for washing, and from Kochevar's Saloon for drinking and cooking.

"My great-grandfather owned the home, but he didn't build it. Maybe some day it will all be straightened out," he concluded.

Fritz went to work in the coal mines in 1924 at the age of eighteen, mining at the Pershing, Buckley, Peanut, and Big Mine for about twenty-eight years. His back was broken in the Peanut Mine, and he was also injured during a roof cave-in at the Big Mine. His already short stature was further diminished by the injuries.

With the passage of Prohibition in 1919, the saloon had been turned into a general store, evidently as a cover since the still was found years later in the workshop in the side

John Tezak, a partner in the Kochevar mink business, on July 4, 1980.
His son John Jr., Trudy's cousin, lived here as a young boy and often returns to visit.

This sign was discovered during the remodeling of Kochevar's in the 1980s.

shed. Fritz had a business of his own there—a pool hall and cigar store, which explained his skill at the game.

Trudy remembers Fritz's mom and dad living in the back part of the saloon.

"Fritz had flaming red hair, as did three of his sisters. And they all had this fine, pale, almost translucent skin," she said. "I was born strawberry blonde, and you can't even see my eyebrows they're so light."

I asked her, "How are you related to Fritz?"

"Let's see . . . Fritz's dad, Jacob, was my great-uncle because he was my grandmother's brother. My dad is Fritz's first cousin, and I am second cousin to Fritz's brothers' kids, so that makes me something once removed." There was a question mark in her voice.

"I don't know how to do that genealogy stuff." She threw up her hands and concluded, "We're just related, that's all."

Which is, of course, what any old-timer will tell you: "Everyone is related to everyone in this town." Just as Nettie Kapushion taught me.

DURING THE WINTER OF 1972 I took the lemon and grapefruit trees to my *Crested Butte Pilot* office, also a south-facing building with dusty windows. I hoped they would feel right at home. My mother came to visit, and we transplanted the grapefruit tree into a garbage can.

White flies attacked the two soon after, killing the lemon tree. In a desperate attempt to save the only tree that survived the infestation, I washed it with soap and hosed it down. But eventually the tree succumbed. I felt like I'd destroyed an antique. Luckily I never had to confess to Fritz.

Fritz died in 1973. He had been ill for a time and wasn't living in Crested Butte. His building sat vacant until 1980, when his brothers Matt and Jake, with locals Nick Lypps and Joe Rous, renovated it back into a bar that maintained the Kochevar 1880s' flavor. The stuffed birds, trophy animals, and buffalo head that Jake had mounted in 1936 still watched from the walls. The chairs were like the originals. Heck, some of them were the originals—round wooden backs with short legs. Red-checkered oilcloth covered the circular tables. The roulette wheel hung on the wall behind the bar. Jacob Sr.'s wedding photo was incorporated into the logo. Jacob's workshop was cleaned out and made into Karolina's Kitchen.

Trudy Yaklich, whose grandparents were Kochevars, jogged her memory in 2005 for details about the mink farm.

Matt and Jake Kochevar live in Golden, Colorado, and come to town for the big holidays—July Fourth and Memorial Day. I can't tell if Matt's hair used to be red, but I've experienced his temper. Jake dresses in an elegant western suit with a string tie, sporting his trimmed, snow-white beard and mustache and looking exactly like his grandfather in the logo.

The managers keep the windows pretty clean now. But over the years the stuffed birds have deteriorated, and many of them have been removed. There's a pool table in what used to be Fritz's bedroom, and sometimes if I close my eyes, I can see Fritz squinting down the cue.

Frances Yaklich

FRANCES KOCHEVAR YAKLICH was Fritz Kochevar's sister and Trudy Yaklich's grandmother.

Trudy related how her grandparents met and married.

"My grandfather Phillip Yaklich was staying at the boarding house on Elk Avenue and fell in love with Frances Kochevar. She might not have even been eighteen. She dropped out of

     THE KOCHEVAR FAMILY

Frances Yaklich in 1978.

school in the sixth grade because she got mad at the teachers. Then she went to work for her sister who was a seamstress. But she was always a reader. She read everything ever written about the Kennedy family.

"Marija and Jacob Kochevar, her parents, almost decreed them to get married," continued Trudy. "But she wanted to have a career. She was a spitfire. Most men sent money home to buy a good Catholic girl from Slovenia or Croatia to be their bride. So Frances' parents considered it good fortune that a local man wanted to marry their daughter."

When the couple wed in 1908, her mother gave them a cow as a wedding present, with which they began the Mountain Glow Dairy. The dairy building, with its distinctive curved façade, stands on the corner of Second Street and Maroon Avenue. Trudy remembers delivering milk by horse-drawn sled with her father, Fritz Yaklich, when she was a child.

"Grandpa Phillip arrived in America with twenty-five cents in his pocket when he was seventeen years old and starting out in Pennsylvania," recalled Trudy. "His name was spelled Jaclić. In 1938 Grandma Frances took her husband back to the old country to see the family. She had saved for the trip twenty-five cents at a time."

Frances died in Crested Butte in 1985.

     THE KOCHEVAR FAMILY

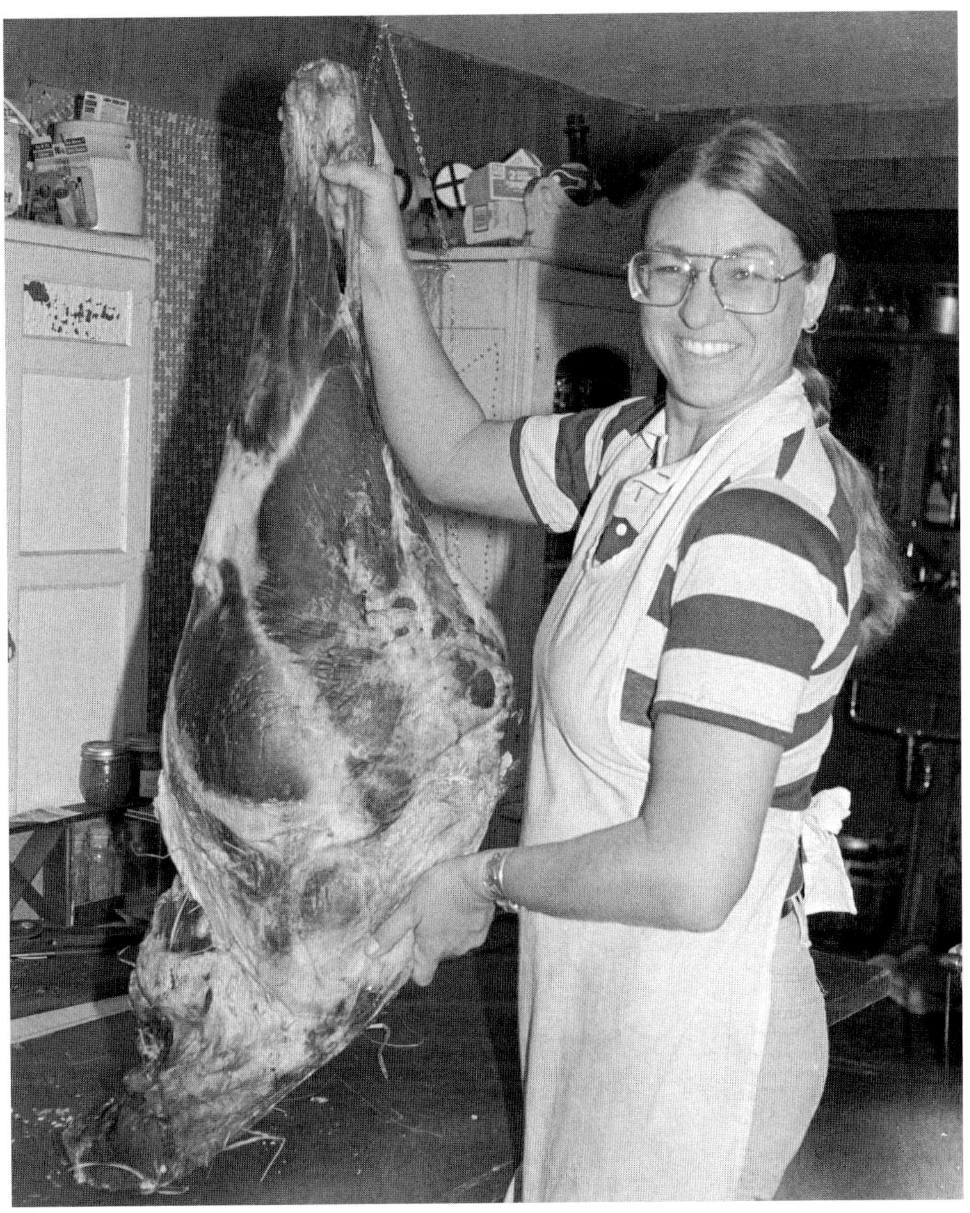

CHAPTER 13

From Trail to Table

Adele Bachman gets ready to butcher the last hindquarter of the elk she shot in 1982.

WINTER, FALL, SPRING, AND SUMMER are the four seasons of the year in most parts of the world. Not in Crested Butte. Here we have ski season, hunting season, mud season, and the Fourth of July.

If you are a meat-eater, hunting season offers a way to "buy" some cheap meat, as long as you don't count your time, effort, and shoe leather, and aren't too squeamish.

During the late 1970s and early 1980s, I was a meat-eater but not a hunter. Thanks to my male friends, however, I found my niche in the meat packers union. I helped to carry out an elk or deer, and in exchange for my labor, received a bag full of steaks, burgers, and ribs, all neatly wrapped in white butcher paper and labeled with black marker. Dependable meat packers were hard to find, especially on a weekday. This was before the days of all-terrain four-wheelers, and few people owned horses. So it wasn't a bad trade-off.

Thus it was that I got a call one Monday. "Can you be ready to pack out in an hour?" It was Craig, my sister's boyfriend.

"What did you get?"

"A five-point bull. Jeff and I spotted him Sunday late afternoon and this morning we were up there by dawn. Got a clean shot, so we didn't have to track him."

"Where at?"

"Jack's Cabin cut-off."

"How far up?"

"Not too far."

I could detect the fudging in his voice. I had been packing out elk enough years to know that "not far" usually meant about two or three miles as opposed to five or six, and most of it uphill.

"We brought out the rack and hindquarters. We've already cut off the head so it won't take much time to load and bring him out."

Oh good, I thought. I hate being there when they cut off the head.

"We'll meet you at one o'clock. We'll be parked at the top, right off the road. Can you recruit any other members of the meat packers union? Maybe your sis wants to come."

Unspoken between us was the knowledge that the fewer people carrying out the meat, the less would have to be given away as payment, leaving more for the hunter. So if he wanted another person, it must be a pretty big elk.

I doubted Kathy would be interested. She was a potter and didn't like being interrupted during her studio work. I underestimated the power of love.

I gave her the short list of all I had learned during past expeditions.

"Wear your grubbiest, brightest [as in orange or red], loosest fitting clothes and warm gloves. But even though they might not be really warm, you'd better wear your wafflestomper hiking boots [with Vibram soles]," I advised. "You won't get chilled until you get back to the truck, and the beer and heater will warm you up pretty fast."

"What about food?" Kathy never went longer than two hours without eating. She claimed she was hypoglycemic; I never believed it for a second.

"Better bring some. It could take us all afternoon."

When we reached the top of Jack's Cabin Cut-Off Road, the guys were loading up for the hike. I hoisted my webbed pack frame. Kathy carried a regular pack with a large inner pocket, no doubt filled with snacks.

After about an hour, "not far" was feeling "real far." We weren't following a trail, just bushwhacking in five inches of snow past the occasional bright surveyor's tape markers Jeff had tied to bushes and trees to guide us to the elk.

Craig tried to make my sister feel more at ease. "It's right up this ravine . . . It's not far now . . . We'll have to take you girls out to dinner."

My breathless reply, "Save the encouragement for when we really need it, like on the way back."

As he passed me, I said to Jeff, "Wish I had your long legs."

"Yeah," he replied with a grin. "But your feet aren't as heavy."

The meat packers union wasn't really an official union—just a description of a group of friends trading muscle for meat, and loosely divided into four classes:

The Plugger—just keeps on truckin' and never seems to tire or talk. Bruce "Face" Newman fits this category, despite his ranting and raving during softball games. It was he—one of the few male non-hunters I knew—who coined the term "meat packers union" as a joke.

The Shirker—brings a small pack and can only carry half an elk backstrap, the prized tenderloin.

The Macho Man—always strides out in front, trying to impress you with his hunting knowledge.

The Squealer—continually complains about how far away from the road we have to hike (see Shirker above).

Determined not to fall into the "squealer" category, I buttoned my lip and kept climbing.

I had my head down and was concentrating on breathing and walking when I caught sight of Jeff a few hundred yards in front of me, rustling through a pile of leaves and sticks. As I approached I could see the elk had already been skinned and partially quartered. Jeff had hidden him in the shady bushes to keep the meat as cool as possible.

I stroked his tan, short-haired hide draped casually on the snow and murmured my thanks for his life. This magnificent animal had endured deep snow, scarce food, and hunters intent only on his huge rack, who might discard the meat and tie the antlers to the cab of their truck, bragging all the way back home—often out of the state. Somehow it seemed especially important to thank this regal bull elk that had cheated death for so long.

Jeff left the head in the brush, for which I was grateful. I didn't want to look at his glassy unseeing eyes. The snow was speckled pink with blood.

Kathy's eyes were wide. All this was new to her except the blood and guts part. She had killed, cleaned, and plucked fowl on her farm and taught me how to pluck 'em fast before rigor mortis set in and the feathers were really hard to get out. After surveying the scene, she sat down and pulled out some food to share—apples, bananas, and energy bars. Squeamish she's not.

During the loading of the packs we went easy on her—it was her initiation to the union. Kathy carried the neck, rib scraps, and all our extra jackets, tools, and saws. She had packed so much food and clothing there was hardly room for the meat.

I ended up with the liver and heart—the delicacies of the animal—wrapped in the heavy hide for insulation, while the fellas each had a front quarter and half the backstrap. It's the long section of tenderloin running across the spine from front shoulder to hind leg, and every good hunter knows that his packers deserve at least one steak out of it.

I felt pretty confident about the hike back until Craig lifted my pack onto my back. "Jeez, Craig, how much does this sucker weigh?" My thirty-eight-year-old knees protested.

"Oh, I'd say about fifty pounds." I think he was fudging again to make me feel better. That was okay because I wanted to feel better about carrying almost half my body weight.

Off we trudged through the snow, under which were lurking slick aspen leaves and downed logs; fifty-plus pounds on your back, and two miles still to go—it's business as usual for the Crested Butte meat packers union. Or so I cheerily told Kathy as I heard her panting behind me.

The side hills were the worst. One false step through the crusty snow and I was sliding downhill the wrong way. My waffle stompers weren't much help. I may as well have opted for toasty toes and worn my everyday winter boots. Every stumble was a brief respite to get my wind. Once, Craig sat down beside me. When my rear end started to freeze, I was ready to get up. Things became a bit tricky. My unsteady thighs shook with the weight of the hide hanging off my back.

"First get down on your hands and knees," suggested Craig. He demonstrated by rolling over from his sitting position into a beetle-like crouch.

"Then you walk up the tree with your hands."

I dutifully followed his lead, and we two beetles inched our way up the rough bark until we were upright. I started to giggle. "Only instead of a shiny, black back, I've got a hairy one."

Then a sobering thought—it's the end of the season, when anyone who hasn't taken an animal can be a bit quick on the trigger finger. We could hear occasional shots in the distance, and with the hide on my back, I'm an elk on two legs. As soon as we get into the open, some nearsighted hunter might get off a shot before he counts the number of legs. I can feel the hair prickle on the back of my neck.

Craig pulled some of the bright orange surveyor's tape out of his pocket and decorated my pack with strips. "We did the same thing this morning when we took out the rack. There's probably nothing to worry about in the trees, though." He tried to reassure me.

We silently plodded on. Kathy, with the lightest pack, had caught up with the long-legged Jeff. The cold beer waiting back at the pickup and the knowledge that Jeff would come back after unloading his pack and take over mine kept me going. Three hundred yards short of the truck, I gratefully handed over my burden.

Several weeks later my friend Adele Bachman asked me to come over and feast on elk heart, tenderloin, and liver. Since I was still waiting for the bag of meat from the guys, I accepted eagerly. Adele is a fabulous cook—an earth mother with brains. The Crested Butte town finance officer, she was raising her thirteen-year-old daughter, Genevieve, by herself. I thought she was brilliant. I thought *anyone* who could understand accounting and numbers was brilliant.

A tall, big-boned woman, she enfolded me in a bear hug when I arrived with my offering of red wine.

The meal was superb, complemented with wild chanterelle mushrooms she had picked herself.

"It wasn't hard to cook. About all you need to do to the heart, liver, and tenderloin is sauté them in butter and onions and mushrooms. But you mustn't overcook them," she cautioned. "Medium rare!"

"Is this from Brekke's elk?" I asked. Her boyfriend was working that night, so it was just we ladies.

"Nope, I got it myself!" Knowing how capable Adele was, I wasn't too surprised, but I *was* totally in awe.

When I left, I paid her my ultimate compliment. "That was better than my mother's absolute finest meal."

"Would you like to leave me a tip for it?" Her gray-blue eyes crinkled at the corners.

"Sure, what's fair?"

"How about helping me butcher the last hindquarter over the weekend? It needs to hang in my shed another few days. Plus I have to work until then."

The following Saturday, Adele, Genevieve, and I sat around her kitchen table. It was covered with a clean cloth and held two sturdy wooden chopping boards. While she deftly wielded a knife, slicing off steaks, I worked on what would become stew meat—cutting off fat and making bite-sized portions. It was my first time butchering, so I was glad not to do anything too complicated. Genevieve wrapped the meat in white butcher paper and labeled each package.

"Okay, now tell me how you got this elk," I said.

The tale of "Adele, the Great White Huntress," as I called her only half in jest, unfolded.

"I was hunting with the county planner and a lady friend from Delta on the other side of Kebler Pass and spotted a herd. Some other hunters flushed it, and a spike elk [a one-year-old bull] was coming straight at me. I shot him in the neck but had to chase through the brush after him and across the creek. Two other hunters I didn't know followed me. They finished him off when we caught up with him."

"How come you didn't put the final bullet in it?" I asked.

"I was shaking too much," she replied. "I'm not used to running a quarter of a mile after an elk." Adele played catcher on our softball team but was prized more for her ability to rattle the batter than to beat the throw to home plate.

"Wow, I'm impressed!"

"I really still believe I haven't done anything anyone else couldn't do if they wanted to." She shrugged.

"You didn't call the meat packers union." I pretended to be offended.

"We gutted it and then had to drag it across a very deep meadow stream, but luckily didn't have to go very far to the truck. The one that was a bitch was the cow elk I shot on Mt. Axtell once. She was way up the basin, and it took Jeff and his brother seven hours to drag her out on foot, downhill on the snow."

"How'd you learn to butcher like that?" I wanted to know.

"I learned a lot from my dad. And you're not going to believe this, but also from *The Joy of Cooking.*"

　　　　　　　　FROM TRAIL TO TABLE

"No!"

"Yes. If you'd look beyond the cookie and pie section where you hang out you'll see the part on game—here, you need a sharper knife for that fat. And don't go cutting any fingers."

It wasn't funny then, but we could laugh now at the memory of the time I cut into a round of cheddar cheese with a fancy knife at a fancy cocktail party and ended up in the emergency room for stitches in three fingers.

"So why did you go for an elk? There's got to be an easier way to get meat for the winter."

"Economics. That's all. I figure this bull elk cost me $80. And I got 150 pounds of meat. It's worth it, even with all the work."

I calculated her time as best I could—three of us were spending a day doing just one quarter; the other quarters had already been butchered, plus the backstrap, rib meat, neck meat . . . lots of hours, and Adele could only do it on weekends or evenings. But I knew better than to question her arithmetic. Besides, she probably couldn't estimate the "pride in accomplishment" factor.

"I had no idea you could shoot."

"I learned from my two older brothers when I was younger than Genevieve. I used to be such a good shot in high school that my cousins stopped taking me rabbit hunting. Guess they didn't want to be shown up by a girl." Adele threw back her head and laughed heartily.

TWENTY YEARS LATER Genevieve shot her first elk. Adele told me she has natural talent. "But when she was hunting with her cousin and his friends, she had the same experience I had. Her cousins didn't like her out-shooting them."

Genevieve is a midwife, soft-spoken, gentle and tall and beautiful enough to be a model. She met her mother's boyfriend out at a friend's ranch, and fired Adele's .270 just to sight it in and get used to it.

"She shot twice, dropped the cow with a bullet to the head, and lost no meat," reported Adele during our e-mail exchange. Her pride sparkled across the wires. A hunter shows her true skill by taking an animal without ruining any steaks.

I turned in my meat packers union card long ago. My knees forced me to quit after Jeff and Craig's elk. Today my husband and I awaken in our home high in the forest and thrill to find ourselves surrounded by one hundred elk pawing the snow for frozen blades of grass. They watch us through our large windows like *we're* the animals in the zoo. Wary but unafraid, they know they are safe in the front yard of a *former* member of the meat packers union.

I miss them at the dinner table, but they have rewarded me with their majestic presence. Not a bad trade-off. And I'd rather enjoy them alive than carry them dead.

CHAPTER 14

"Play Ball!"

1970–1985

Martin "Pitsker" Sporcich in 1968 warms the bench in front of Frank and Gal's.

I WAS SOCKED IN THE CHEST with a batted ball at age fourteen during a game with the boys and slunk home in pain and embarrassment. So why was I was on first base ten years later hollering, "Hey batter, batter, batter!"?

Sometime between the 1950s when the mines closed and the early 1970s when I found myself on first, no one was playing much softball or baseball. Many families had left Crested Butte; those that stayed either didn't have the inclination or time, or perhaps enough players to make up two teams.

I asked my neighbor Lyle McNeill about it: "Lyle, didn't you guys ever play baseball growing up?"

"Well, sure we did. The outfield fence was located just inside my parents' property, close to Fifth Street and Sopris, and we were the only kids allowed to sit on the fence. They chased everyone else off," the former mayor recalled with a chuckle.

Then I checked with Rudy Sedmak, Lyle's schoolmate, who said, "Baseball was a big thing in Crested Butte. You could get any job you wanted if you were a good player."

In the late 1960s, Crested Butte, with its many vacant lots covered with patchy weeds and grass, was ripe for "sandlot" ball. It wasn't long before we had scared up enough people for a couple of softball teams.

The field was across the highway from Lyle's and my homes and eventually became the Town Park. At first it was a rough unbordered area of dirt and rocks. Second basemen were plagued by a knob about ten feet in front of the base that, if it caught a groundball just right, would send it zigging while the baseperson zagged.

When a left-handed big hitter like Jerry Heal came to bat, the whole outfield shifted to their left. The right fielder sighed in resignation. He knew he'd have to root around in the thick, scratchy willows on the west side of the field before emerging with the ball, which was invariably a home run. Left-field home runs were apt to strike a passing car. If the hit made it over the road without bouncing off the hood, the left fielder had it almost as bad as the right fielder.

From my back yard I could watch him trot across the road and start beating the high weeds near the edge of the vacant lot separating my house from the highway and the softball diamond. If I had seen the ball land, I'd stroll over and point it out to him. Otherwise I'd sit back and enjoy the show, especially when the center fielder came out to help him search.

Outfield fences and a backstop were nonexistent. The teams sat on a pair of benches, one on each side of the field. The fans made do with the rocky dirt on the sidelines. Best of all, no one remembered, or particularly cared, what the score was.

As casual Sunday afternoon pick-up games gave way to more serious men's and women's league play, the softball players needed a dependable umpire. In the course of conversation at the local bars, someone discovered that old-timer and ex-miner Martin "Pitsker" Sporcich had done a little ball-playing during his sixty-odd years.

"Hey, Pitsker," asked one of players, "would you help us out on the softball field?"

"I might umpire a game or two," he said.

One of the guys each game day looked Pitsker up at Tony's Tavern, the Grubstake, or Frank and Gal's where he was enjoying a beer, and drove him to the field so he could "umpire a game or two."

The old bachelor's needs were simple: "I need a ride to and from the field, 'cause my legs just aren't what they used to be, and a six-pack to keep my whistle wet."

From somewhere, a mask and later a chest protector appeared. Pitsker stuck a well-worn whiskbroom in his back pocket, and after the runner slid into home, he pushed his mask up and ceremoniously bent over to sweep the dusty plate. Slowly, he straightened, donned the mask, and let loose with a resounding "Play ball!"

At least once during each game he would eye a bobbled pitch rolling across home plate, shakily raise his gnarly, arthritic hand, and boom, "Steerike!" The pitcher's face lit up. The opposing team groaned. But "kill the ump" was not in our vocabulary. A six-pack was hardly a full-time paycheck.

To make up for his error later in the game, Pitsker gave the benefit of the doubt to a batter on the "wronged" team. A pitch just inside the strike zone would be called a "ball."

His nieces were somewhat dubious about his abilities as an umpire.

"Uncle Martin is blind, I swear it," one told her team.

"That's right, he can't see at all. No way is he going to know a ball from a strike," insisted her sister.

"Absolutely true," added a third sister.

"He used to be an excellent carpenter." They were all in agreement about that. "But knowing a ball from a strike? Hah."

Maybe eyeballing the ball wasn't a whole lot different than eyeballing measurements. During that first beer, he was pretty darned accurate. In any event, he was the sole person you could depend on to umpire those hot, dusty doubleheaders on Saturdays when the teams and spectators consumed a keg of beer, and Pitsker drank two instead of his usual one six-pack. And he never gave a break on a called ball or strike to any of his nieces, reinforcing his reputation for fairness.

The names of the teams reflected the laid-back attitudes of the earthy 1970s—Breasted Buttes, Loaded Ladies, Mountain Mamas, Ruthless Babes, One-Eyed Trouser Snakes, Chumps, Sore Losers, and my championship team one year, the Ballbusters.

It was serious, but not too serious. How can you take a team named the Trouser Snakes seriously? The Snakes' dubious claim to fame was "The Face," a skinny elastic guy with a rubber arm on third base. Despite his reputation as a poker-faced card shark, a trait that had earned him his nickname, his emotions were front and center when it came to softball. He acknowledged the cheers from the sidelines, usually the ladies, making a big show of brushing off the dust after snagging a line drive on his belly.

Pitsker calls 'em as he sees 'em in 1974.

Micky Cooper, in 1979, fields a grounder while the runner gets by.
Old snow fence from the ski area encircles the field.

It was his erratic hitting ability that frustrated him. After each pop-up he'd throw the bat down in disgust. "Oh man, I'm the worst!" After slamming a home run he'd turn with a triumphant grin, both arms raised. "Who's the best!" And he'd jog around the bases, high-fiving his teammates down the third-base line.

Before the town got rich enough to hire a recreation director, Trouser Snakes pitcher Mark Calve provided the game schedules and scores to the newspapers, and bought the keg, being reimbursed at twenty-five cents per paper cup from team members and spectators. His most important responsibility was seeing Pitsker safely home after the double-header. He also pitched a mean change-up ball for the Snakes, and excelled at chasing stray dogs out of the infield.

"No dogs, man!" he'd bellow to the sheepish owner of an offender who broke the unwritten "no dogs, no bottles" rule.

About the only costs back then were the printing of team T-shirts and the beer. If you had any spare change, kneepads, cleated shoes, and team ball caps were luxury purchases. But we were always short of practice balls and good bats.

At first skills were rusty, and errors counted for a lot, especially in the women's games—the team making the least amount of them usually won. It resulted in such high scores, however, that eventually the ten-run rule was enacted. If one team was winning by more than ten runs when the fifth inning rolled around, the game was officially over, although the teams could keep playing by mutual consent—just for practice.

Not that there weren't some hot women players. During one triple play, I watched the shortstop catch a pop fly, tag one player halfway to third, and throw the other out at second.

     "PLAY BALL!"

My mother, who became our relief pitcher, takes a little batting practice in 1977.

One summer as the teams started to form, our regular pitcher warned the rest of the ladies, "I'm pregnant. I won't be able to play later in the summer, so you'd better find some-one—"

"Pregnant! Not at this time of year. Why didn't you wait till winter?" demanded our catcher, who had already gotten that baby stuff out of the way.

"Well, ladies, it can't be helped. I'll be back next summer. You can handle it for one year."

A couple of our teammates tried pitching during the next few practices, but it soon became evident that none of them could fill the void. Back then, if you didn't have a pitcher, you didn't have a team.

"It's looking bleak," moaned the catcher. "Real bleak."

"Let me try it." My shy mother, here for the summer and an occasional substitute, held out her hand for the ball.

I knew she had been athletic earlier in her life. But like many kids, I found it hard to imagine my parents ever being young, not to mention proficient in a sport. Our scrapbook has an old photograph of her in a dance performance. But softball pitcher? I was having trouble with it. And she was old—forty-five.

Nonetheless, she started pitching, and each toss got better and better. The next game, she was the starter, our savior. We would not be in championship contention that summer, but I enjoyed incredulous comments from other players. "That's your mother? No way."

As we got older, with a few more seasons under our belts and more and more scheduled games, we women wearied of the bickering over umpire calls and putdowns of teammates who made errors. We just wanted to play ball, drink beer, and have fun.

Paul Hitchcock grabs the practice ball
Pam Smith hid under her T-shirt in 1981.

By then, other players were relieving Pitsker when the game load got to be too heavy. I could hear the arguing over calls all the way to my back door.

My team that summer was the Wong Way/Gears, sponsored by a bar/restaurant, the Way Station, owned by the Wong family, and Gears, a heavy equipment company. Right from the beginning we laid down the law to the coaches: If you yell at anyone, you're fired. In addition, everyone who shows up for the game gets to play.

Sure, it was best to play the same ladies on the infield each game. We got tight, we got good. But the Wong Way/Gears, in our quest for a good time, recruited women who were comfortable playing several positions. That way there were no recriminations if you had to miss a practice or a game. We were out for a good time, not pressure. The twenty-seven women on the roster that summer of 1982 sat out a couple of innings each game so someone else could play.

I was usually on first base because I throw like a girl. I could catch anything, though, so I almost never had to throw farther than to the pitcher. And if I concentrated, I was usually accurate, though not very fast. Despite my throwing shortfalls, we won the championship and were treated to a boisterous evening of champagne toasts at Wong's Way Station.

One season while women in other cities were burning bras in their quest for equality, I asked my friend Dave, only half in jest, "What about a coed team? It'd be fun."

By then I think many of the men were also sick of the bickering. "Sure, Sandy, I'll ask Clayton and a couple of the boys," he said, to my amazement. He got five guys, and I came up with six gals. Men and women alternated positions and Dave pitched.

"I've got bad news for you," said Mark Calve. "The guys are afraid to play your team 'cause they don't think the girls can handle the fast pitches, and the women's teams don't want to play you 'cause they think you'll be too good."

We didn't play too many games that summer.

In 1984 I left for a year at acting school, and when I returned softball was losing its magic. The games were scheduled two per night *except* weekends. Everyone got married and had babies, and weekends were for weddings, the kids, or to get out of town, not for softball and beer. Chain link replaced the rickety snow fence around the field. Netting went up to intercept the homers headed for the highway.

"PLAY BALL!"

Pitsker's legs, never strong to begin with, had given out in 1976, but not before a back-stop and bleachers were built, and a wooden sign, naming the field in his honor, was erected. For many years he only umped the championship game. Then he was relegated to throwing out the first ball of the season. The town hired a full-time umpire, paying him in cash, not beer.

Winning became more important than the fun of playing, or the thrill of your first home run. Fair pitches used to be whatever you could consistently get over the plate. Now it's slow pitch only with the ump judging the arc of the ball. Coed teams are the norm.

By 1985 the once rocky field, now a dim memory, had been sodded and is now kept pristinely green by an underground sprinkler system that turns on every morning, rain or shine; the dandelions are regularly sprayed with poison from the same tractor that mows the field once a week. The driver wears a white suit and a respirator. The recreation director pushes a little cart to chalk the base lines before each game.

And the once thirty-something, now forty- and fifty-something, crowd nurses ski injuries and sits for grandbabies. The Snakes no longer field a team—the Face left town. Pitsker turned eighty-six and up and died on us in 1992.

And me? Well, I keep my mitt, kneepads, bat, and ball handy, just in case.

Tony Mihelich was one of the best ball players Crested Butte had ever seen. He was scouted by the big leagues, but chose to "pitch" seeds at his Crested Butte Hardware instead of baseballs.

CHAPTER 15

Willard Ruggera

Willard Ruggera, his mother Sophie, and her dog, CoCo, in 1986.

WILLARD RUGGERA is Crested Butte's only remaining World War II veteran, and at age eighty-two and a half, he could still button his uniform jacket and march in the 2003 Memorial Day parade out to the cemetery. He's got most of his hair, and the best of his health. A "glass is half full" attitude keeps him looking on the bright side. I figured an interview of my favorite polka partner and a few photographs were in order.

Willard's mother, Sophia Beitler Ruggera, of German ancestry, was born here in 1897; his father, Felice, was from northern Italy. Willard was born in Crested Butte on December 7, 1921, in a little stucco-sided house on the corner of Gothic Avenue and Second Street.

"I can't speak either Italian or German, although I can understand some words," he said. "But Ronnie [his wife] can speak Croatian." As it turns out, Ronnie's mother, Veronika Stimac, was born in Croatia and was my family's next-door neighbor when we arrived in 1964. I've never forgotten her welcoming loaf of bread on our kitchen table.

Willard's family didn't always live in Crested Butte. His parents spent a few years at the top of Smith Hill, four miles from town, where his dad was the hoist operator at the mine.

"My mom skied my brother down on skis to school and rode the ore car on the hoist back up to the mine," Willard said.

He and his five siblings (a sixth died shortly after birth) then moved to a ranch at the confluence of Muddy and Lee Creeks on the south side of McClure Pass. Willard rode on horseback behind his older brother to attend a country school there for his first two months of first grade.

"It was one where all the grades were taught by one teacher," he explained.

Deciding that he needed to continue his schooling in Crested Butte, Willard's parents sent him here to live with his aunt and uncle Gulliford. Willard had appendicitis two months later and eventually had to repeat the first grade.

"Back then they didn't do surgery for that very often. It was pretty risky. Dr. Alfred, who was an army surgeon but worked for Colorado Fuel and Iron [CF&I], gave me this weird diet—white gelatin, broth, and no water—I could only suck on icicles. They gave me morphine shots and put this brown paper on my stomach," he recalled. "Anyway, I've never had my appendix taken out. Back then it didn't cost anything. CF&I took care of everything if your dad was a miner."

From those days, Willard has an odd assortment of memories.

"Auntie Annie had a Model-T Ford, one of the first to have one [in town]," he said. "Of course, back then almost everyone put their cars up on blocks for the winter. They took out the battery and took off the wheels to save the tires. They didn't plow the streets in the 1920s, so you didn't need a car. Everyone took the train," he added, "or walked."

His parents returned to Crested Butte when Willard entered the third grade. And his dad went back to the mines. Almost without exception the Crested Butte men spent their lives working in the coal mines. But Willard was an exception.

"I wanted to fly. I wanted to be an army pilot."

It took a while to win his wings. First, during his high school summers, Willard put in his time at the Peanut Mine, known then as the Horace Anthracite, where his uncle Fred Gulliford was the boss. The summer he graduated, Willard went by bus to Chanute Field in Illinois, hoping to fulfill his dream.

"I thought it was a pilot school, but it turned out to be a technical school—more about repairing planes, so I came home and went to work in the Big Mine with my dad and his friend Charlie Tezenbacker.

"I was in the third level. It was the worst. Rock falling all the time. We were digging pick coal. All the time bent over. It was such a low entry they had to use mules to pull the ore cars out to the hoist and up to the tipple. Some of the big cars held twenty-one tons. We used to ride out in the empty cars. It was a mile and a half in.

"One day I was working with Barney Niccoli and Will Kapushion and my dad, and we're just sitting there having lunch when a slab of rock fell down and knocked off our helmets.

"'The hell with this,' we said. 'Let's go join the army. Sure, they shoot at you, but at least you can shoot back.'"

Pearl Harbor was bombed on Willard's twenty-first birthday; he and Barney drove to Denver and enlisted in 1942. He had spent only nine months in the coal mines and never went back.

For three and one-half years he was in an armored division out of Ft. Benning, Georgia.

"I worked on inspections of tanks and half-tracks before they were sent overseas."

Despite his German heritage, Willard held no love for the Nazis, "although I kind of admired the way they were dressed—in black and all." He grinned, waiting to see if I'd fall for it.

Veronika Stimac, Ronnie Ruggera's mother, ventured out to watch the 1978 Fourth of July parade.

"I watched the paratroopers train, and I thought I'd like to do that. But my company commander talked me out of it. He said if you got shot behind enemy lines, you were in the infantry all by yourself." So Willard drove tanks and transports in France in the Third Army under General George S. Patton.

Following his discharge he worked at the CF&I filling station on the corner of Third Street and Elk Avenue. Then he went to work at the CF&I Company Store.

"I didn't want to go back to the mine!" He shook his head, remembering.

During this time Ronnie, whom Willard had dated a few times in high school, was attending the Barnes Business College in Colorado Springs.

"He wrote letters to me all the time," said Ronnie. "I was so homesick. I thought, 'What a great guy writing me all these letters!'" They wed on June 4, 1946; shortly thereafter, Ronnie started working as the secretary-treasurer for the nascent Rural Electric Association. And then the children started to come—every three years. First was Vicki in 1947, then Michael, Diane, Elaine, Wayne, and Karen.

Willard never stopped dreaming about flying, however. The passage of the GI Bill, whereby the federal government paid for further education for veterans, helped make his dream come true. In Willard's case, this meant flying lessons. Since Willard had already been hired as Crested Butte town manager in 1948, he didn't feel the urge to go on to college on the GI Bill as his brother did, so instead, during his time off from the town, he learned to fly from Rocky Warren in Gunnison.

Rocky, a former army pilot and instructor, owned a flying school and charter service in Gunnison called Western State Aviation.

"He was a great mountain flyer," said Willard. "He was one of the best!"

Rocky's main business was aerial photography. A big, jovial guy, he was elected Gunnison County commissioner in 1980.

During his training Willard flew to Ohio and California, or "sometimes to Grand Junction for coffee. I'd call up Ronnie and she'd say, 'Where are you?'" Ronnie knew if he was close by, he probably wouldn't be calling.

"We flew those tail skidders—single engines—and I landed at Stapleton [Airport] in Denver without a radio. Back then they had lights mounted on the outside of the tower, like a stoplight. If they gave you a green light, it was OK to land. The red light meant you had to go around again. You still had to keep an eye out for traffic. But it was a small airport back then. And there were no jets.

"Ronnie kept saying, 'One of these days you're going to get killed.' So after the GI Bill ran out, I gave it up. I couldn't afford to pay for it myself, anyway." By then, explained Willard, the town manager job entailed even more work following the resignation of the town clerk, Mark Byouk.

"I had to do everything. I made $180 a month. The town had no money. The Big Mine had paid $125 a month for town water and $35 a month for the water tank [now dismantled]. When the mines closed [and the CF&I money dried up], the main revenue was the

*Veronica "Ronnie" Ruggera in 1982. In addition to raising their five children,
Ronnie was the town's only day care provider during the 1960s and '70s, often
watching over seven or eight children in their home from eight to five, five days a week.*

water bills—you paid $7 every three months if you had a bathroom, otherwise it was $4.50. The town got $4,200 of an 80-mill levy. And I also had to collect the liquor license fees. Frank Starika, the mayor then, used to pay for his license in 375 silver dollars. He'd give them to me in a fishing case, and I had to haul the heavy thing to Gunnison. There was no bank here back then."

Part of his job was thawing the water lines that ran under the streets. The Elk Avenue line was only three or four feet deep. Because the insulating snow was being plowed off the road, the pipe was always freezing. Residents would let their water run, and the low pressure in the main would exacerbate the problem. As the town water lines were replaced, they were buried six to seven feet deep in the alleys, which were not plowed. Even now Willard cringes when he hears about plowing alleys. "They can still freeze," he warned.

As he and Ronnie added to their family, Willard had his eye out for extra work, and on the side he continued to play his saxophone. In high school he had been in the orchestra and the marching band. Later he played both alto and tenor sax with the Salinger Band, and the Roy John McCabe Band, and occasionally sat in with Bill Bailey's band.

After the war he started his own Ruggera Band.

"We practiced in this house." He gestured toward his living room, where his two saxophones and a music stand are set up. Model warplanes are suspended from the ceiling. "Crested Butte had better bands than Gunnison's," he noted.

One of his saxophones is a Selmer, one of the best and oldest names, and most expensive. I admired its gold filigree and told him it was the same make as my husband's.

"Really? Well, it's worth a lot of money."

Next to Ronnie, music is one of Willard's great loves. But it wasn't a full-time profession.

Although he was never crazy about the town manager job, said Willard, "I had kids to feed." So, on the side, Willard went into business with Fritz Yaklich.

"We bought a second-hand backhoe and just learned how to run it by getting out and practicing. With the town, I fixed lines for free. Now we could charge. And we never had to advertise. We did water lines, Forest Service campgrounds, and outhouses." He quit his job as town manager in 1961 after fourteen and one-half years and began working with Fritz full time.

The pair hung out with Rudy Sedmak, who was by then the maintenance man for Dr. Smith and his Law Science Academy. They all took turns playing practical jokes on each other, like the time Willard found a brassiere and put it in Fritz's car.

"Luckily Trudy, Fritz's daughter, found it before his wife did," recalled Rudy. "Or the time Fritz and I were driving back from Gunnison," said Willard, "and there was this horrible smell in the truck. Rudy had stuck Limburger cheese on the back of the heater."

Both Rudy and Willard remember vividly a bucket of water laced with old antifreeze that Fritz and Willard had balanced over the door of the Academy Arms [now the Forest Queen].

Fritz Yaklich in 1978, Willard's partner and Trudy's dad.

Willard's fellow musician Joe Saya in 1981.

"Rudy opened the door, and the bucket fell all over him and his new pair of overalls," said Willard with a slightly chastened grin. "Oh, we were jokers."

On the serious side, Willard was the first Crested Butte representative to the RE 1-J School Board, formed in the 1960s when the Crested Butte School lost its autonomy and the town's children were bused to Gunnison High School. It was an unpopular decision that Willard fought, to no avail.

Now that Willard's retired, he and Ronnie, who have been married sixty years, enjoy their children, five grandchildren, and three great-grandchildren. They spend part of the year in Boston, Massachusetts, near three of their children—Karen, Wayne, and Elaine—and half the year in Colorado near the other three; Vicki, married to Shammy Somrak Jr., lives outside of Gunnison, and Mike and Diane live in Denver. Willard keeps two of his saxophones in Boston, where he plays for senior groups. In Crested Butte, he occasionally joins accordion players Chris Rouse and Pete Dunda.

Each summer Willard and Ronnie relax in their grassy, tree-lined yard bordered by thick bunches of prickly raspberry bushes.

"These were brought from my folks' ranch on the Muddy many years ago," Willard told me. "Look how they've spread." And we finished our interview, staining our fingers red as we picked and savored the heirloom raspberries.

Joe Saya

BORN OCTOBER 14, 1905, Joe Saya began a thirty-year career as a miner at age seventeen, earning $4.35 a day at the Pershing Mine near Peanut Lake. Mining was his living, but music was his love. He formed a band called "The Merrymakers," later named "Joe Saya and his Orchestra." Joe played saxophone; Joe Vilitti, the accordion; John Pasic, the trumpet; Joe Beitler, the drums; Sis Gulliford, the piano; and Lawrence Perko, sax and banjo. The group played for dances every weekend in surrounding towns, including Montrose, Paonia, and Durango. Each member was paid $5 per night for making music from 9 p.m. to 2 a.m. with only a half-hour intermission at midnight.

"My first love was the banjo," Joe recalled. "I ordered one from the Sears-Roebuck catalog for $12. It sounded just like hitting bailing wire." And he laughed with that quick smile that I found so difficult to capture on film.

Joe married Pauline in 1936, and they raised three children: Joe Jr., Robert, and Joyce. Joe Jr. comes often to stay in the family home on Maroon Avenue, with its back yard a profusion of pink Oriental poppies, roses, columbines, delphiniums, and raspberries. Joyce lives with her husband, Rix Rixford, in Gunnison. Joe died August 14, 1992.

CHAPTER 16

Christmas in Crested Butte, 1980s Style

Annie Perko in 1974. We often began our cross-town Christmas caroling at her house.

CHRISTMAS AND MY BIRTHDAY have been intertwined all my life. I love Christmas. But having been born four days before the big day, as a child I felt cheated. "Here's your combined birthday and Christmas present," said my sisters. One present, not two like everyone else. Because school was on break, I never got a classroom party like the rest of the kids. And when I discovered that December 21 was the winter solstice, the shortest day of the year, my misery was complete. Or so I thought, until I moved to Crested Butte. In a ski resort, not only is my birthday overlooked, but the whole town is crazy busy the two weeks before, during, and after Christmas Day.

Depending on their jobs, Crested Butteans celebrate Christmas during their off-hours. Chairlift operators work Christmas Day. A dishwasher might never make it to the Christmas Eve service at the church. Restaurant owners don't see the light of day until almost the second week in January. Bus drivers, shop owners, maids—same story. And a December 21 birthday really goes by the wayside.

One highlight of the holiday season was caroling night, sometime the week before Christmas, when action at the resort and in town was just revving up. Whenever I was involved in the planning of a caroling party, I piped up, "Let's have it on the twenty-first."

"Sure, why not?" came the reply. The date didn't really matter, of course—except to me, the birthday girl, looking for a party—any party.

Some years just a group of friends went; other years it was more organized, usually by the choirs of the Union Congregational Church or the Oh-Be-Joyful Church. When it comes to caroling, however, religious affiliation becomes unimportant. What counts is whether you can carry a tune. And do you have a flashlight, or access to a copy machine to make up twenty sheets of music?

We had two main goals: singing at old-timers' houses before bedtime, usually by eight o'clock; and making it to all the bars, especially the classy ones whose management would offer the cold singers a hot buttered rum or chocolate after the serenade. Another important goal, at least in my mind, was warbling the obligatory two verses of "Silent Night" without flatting notes or slowing the beat to yawning between phrases. It was best to do "Silent Night" early in the evening, before the cold froze our lips and momentum. It also helped to sing while walking. It's impossible to walk slowly when it's ten degrees out. As you speed up to keep warm, so does the musical tempo.

At each stop, one of us blew what he or she thought might be the correct note on the pitch pipe; then we did two verses of two songs and left them begging for encores. We exited with "We Wish You a Merry Christmas," a song everyone remembered the words to without having to consult the cheat sheet by flashlight. Some people tried to press Christmas cookies on us; others just applauded and loved it. After a final drink it was home to nurse the sore throat, the result of too many tunes started on too many low notes in the icy air.

We often began our cross-town journey by caroling at a home where we knew we would be most welcome—usually a bachelor or widowed old-timer: Annie Perko's sunporch/ mudroom with her blooming African violets, Teeny Tezak's steamy kitchen, or Frank Orazem's front porch on Elk Avenue.

My most vivid caroling birthday of all was singing at John Panian's Sopris Avenue home. John was a crusty old retired miner, stooped over from years of shoveling coal, who could be downright gruff at times, until you got to know him. We didn't expect much of a reception, but we were fresh, so it seemed as good as any place to start. We sang respectfully in front of the darkened house and turned to leave after the two verses. Suddenly the front door opened.

He poked his head out into the cold and beckoned to us. "Come around back. Come inside." We demurred politely. "No. Come around back," he insisted in his husky accented voice. He shut the door. We trooped through the snow around to the back door, where he'd turned on a porch light, and he waved all twelve or fifteen of us in. "Come in, come in!"

I don't think any of us had ever been inside before, but there we were crowding into the tiny old kitchen, wet jackets steaming, boots tracking in snow. The welcome warmth of the

John Panian and my sister Kathy in 1968.

coal stove fogged up some eyeglasses. So we chose a simple carol we'd already memorized. Our audience of one sat down at his little table. As we sang, he smiled beatifically, revealing handsome white false teeth. Tears welled in his eyes and began a slow trickle down his wrinkled cheeks.

During the 1980s I sang in the choir of the 100-year-old Union Congregational Church. The choir leader worked the night nursing shift at the Gunnison hospital, and she and her husband were stretched thin raising two young children. But she was dedicated to her music, and every Monday night, as she led us in song, rehearsing for the Christmas Eve service, the notes slowly wiped the exhaustion from her face.

Marcia Flagg, the young minister, was a singer herself and liberally sprinkled every service with songs. Christmas Eve got a double dose. She said a prayer; we sang two songs. She said another prayer; we sang two songs. A soloist (sometimes me) gave us all a break. Marcia gave a short sermon; we sang two songs.

The finale was the lighting of little white candles, stuck in cardboard holders to protect hands from dripping wax. Everyone in the church had received one on the way in. The house lights went out, and volunteers lit the candle of the first person in each row, who in turn lit their neighbor's, passing the light from candle to candle. It was a breathtaking sight from the choir's vantage point in front, facing the congregation—upturned, happy faces illuminated by flickering candles in the dark church. Marcia blessed us and cautioned everyone about fire, and we all carefully filed out to "Silent Night," sung EVER so slowly, and ALL five verses. At the door we blew out our candles and put them in a box.

This service was so popular with locals and visitors alike that there was a repeat performance at eight o'clock. Marcia really packed them in. Kids sat at the feet of the organist, on the stairs of the altar, and under the Christmas tree that touched the high ceiling.

One Christmas, as the choir took our first breath for "O Holy Night," the town's fire siren pierced the air. An audible gasp, complete silence, and then pagers started going off. EMTs and fire volunteers dashed down the aisles and out the door to the fire department hall a block up the street.

We sang as loudly as we could to mask the continuing alarm. When it finally stopped we looked at each other, a silent, fearful question on each of our faces. "Is it my house or yours? Not on Christmas Eve, please."

The alarm sounded a second time, jolting us out of our thoughts. The organist's notes blended with the shrieking horns of the fire trucks. Only after the service (in which we were oh-so-careful with the little white candles) did we learn that fire had engulfed the Eccher barn on the west edge of town. The following year the fire department organized a barn raising and helped the Ecchers rebuild.

In some ways, Christmas is just another day in a busy ski season, another day in the life of a firefighter or EMT. I always got a kick out of riding with a visitor on the ski lift who asked me, "What's going to be open Christmas Day? When will they open the lifts?" I was working as a hostess for the ski area, so I phrased my reply with care. "Of course, everything will be

The Lacy brothers operated a sleigh ride business in the winter of 1973.
Their route passed the Union Congregational Church.

open as usual. I'll be celebrating my Christmas and birthday December 28 and 29 on my days off."

In other ways, Christmas is more special because there isn't much time to savor it, and it's particularly sweet when celebrated as part of the Crested Butte community. No after-Christmas sales, mobbed malls, and traffic jams for us.

On my own as a young adult in Crested Butte, my birthday and Christmas perceptions changed. Presents I received no longer meant as much. Presents I gave—gifts of music—became more important.

I was growing up. And, as my girlfriends were fond of pointing out with a wink, December 21 is not only the shortest day of the year, it's the longest night.

*Tim Morgan in 1980. Along with Lyle McNeill, Tim and his wife, Helen,
were mainstays of the Union Congregational Church during its early years.
They were named deacons emeritus in 1985 for their service.*

Helen Morgan in 1985. She faithfully played the piano at each service for 55 years.
The Morgans lived across Fourth Street from the church and were its unofficial caretakers.

CHAPTER 17

Betty Spehar,
Growing Up ... Not Old

Betty Spehar in her garden in 1995. I tried unsuccessfully for years to shoot a portrait that I felt did her justice, which is why she is missing from my old-timer collection in the museum. This is her favorite.

O K, BETTY, TELL ME ABOUT this bowling alley at Kochevar's. Did it exist or not?"

Researching a story on the Kochevar family, I'd gotten conflicting reports about the possible existence of a bowling alley in Kochevar's Bar in the early 1900s. But I knew just who to call.

Betty quickly set me straight.

"There was never a bowling alley in Kochevar's, to my knowledge. It was upstairs at Mattivi's in 1936–1940, before Frank and Gal Starika bought it. We bowled after school when I was in high school. It was a big dance hall upstairs and had about four or five lanes. The whole town took an interest in it. We had a ball with it. It was delightful."

Betty Spehar was born in Crested Butte on January 2, 1924. A former Western State College English professor, she's a stickler for accuracy and tells some wonderful tales of growing up in a small mining town. When I need to check the veracity of local legends, she's my woman.

Although I'd known Betty for years as an avid horsewoman, skier, mushroom picker, explorer, and soprano in the choir at the Catholic Church, it wasn't until 1995 that I heard an abbreviated story of her youth. Our two-hour interview for the *Crested Butte Magazine,* which took place in the corner garden of her gently sloping, grassy yard, couldn't begin to cover all that she has done and continues to do, from "touching the shoulder of Mt. Denali in Alaska" to excelling in sports and academia.

Her age and sex never deterred Betty from doing what she wanted. Her favorite words are "delightful," "lovely," and "marvelous." Many years after that interview I still glean treasured bits of local lore from casual conversations with her. She's a living encyclopedia of facts, dates, and stories from her childhood and before. She credits her parents, George and Mary (Mufich), who emigrated from Croatia.

"They were marvelously bright and loved to read and do things with their children. We had magazines, books, newspapers, cultural radio programs like the Sunday afternoon opera, music lessons, and, for the most part, excellent school teachers and programs," said Betty.

"My mother and father lived in Marble, Colorado, before I was born, where my dad and two partners, Ben Jorgenson and Charlie McWilliams, owned the Marble Mercantile," she said.

When the marble quarry shut down in 1916, Betty's family moved to Crested Butte. "Before they made the move," said Betty, "Mother delivered her ultimatum: 'George, do what you want. Go where you want. I just want you to understand I'm never going to move four children and a piano again.'"

In 1926 her father bought the four-unit Pioneer Apartment Hotel on Sopris Avenue, built in 1881.

Betty Spehar's family home, the former Pioneer Apartment Hotel, photographed in 1989.

Explained Betty, "Dad hired some miner friends who spent a year redoing the ground floor. The only qualification, if you owed him a grocery bill and wanted to work to pay it off, was that you be able to hold a hammer and drive a nail. As a result, although most of the workmen were highly qualified, an occasional defect occurred because of the inexperienced friends who were there to put food on the tables during a period when the mine was on a much reduced summer schedule.

"Thereafter, whenever Mom was housecleaning in a major way, which happened twice a year, and she came to a strange bulge in the surface above a door in the living room, if Dad was there, she'd say, 'You and your friends, George!' To his offer to bring someone in immediately and redo the defect, her was reply was always, 'No, I couldn't go through *that* again!'"

With the exception of the practical yellow steel Tevlar siding [a material used on the connections of the Alaskan Pipeline] the Spehar family home looks today much as it did when Betty grew up. It's just down the street from the Catholic Church, where Betty has always been an active member. The mahogany piano, built in 1890, is accorded a place of honor in the parlor. A wagon team hauled it over Schofield Pass to Crested Butte in 1916. A bit of a chore, to say the least, and I could empathize with Mary Spehar's ultimatum to her husband.

As I marveled at all the lovely furniture, Betty was matter-of-fact. "It's a museum of the 1930s, a sentimental shrine. Much of the furniture was made by my brothers in high school classes."

She pointed out the exception, a custom-crafted cabinet by Jacob Kochevar in the kitchen/pantry, and told me, "I'm a history buff, and I just maintain this home the way it was."

After I got the straight skinny about the bowling alley, I asked Betty to make sense of what I term the "saga of the stores." Various historic articles and books refer to several different stores on Elk Avenue. Because her father had owned one of them, she was able to provide the details.

When the Spehars moved from Marble to Crested Butte, George managed his cousin Martin Verzuh's store, located on the site now occupied by the Idle Spur at 226 Elk Avenue. In 1924 George purchased his own general store (started by the Glick brothers in the 1880s.) It was one door east of Verzuh's on the corner of Third Street and Elk Avenue. George's vacant lot separated his store from the next one, which was owned first by Mike Fisher, then by the Byouks, and then by the Stefanics. Betty's story explained the light-colored, clay crock I inherited from my mother that she obtained in the 1960s. Neatly lettered in blue glaze on the side is "Mike Fisher, Wines, Liquors, Cigars, Crested Butte, Colo."

Across the street from all of them was the former Colorado Fuel and Iron's Company Store. In the rear, a small grocery was in operation when we arrived in 1964. With its thick, light-tight door and round panic-bar handle, the meat locker in the butcher department served as my photographic darkroom during the 1970s, long after the grocer had gone out of business.

George sold his store in 1941 to his next-door neighbor John Sporcich, who, with his brother Martin "Pitsker" Sporcich were uncles to all the Sporcich sisters, my next-door neighbors on Elk Avenue. The building was renamed John's Store. By the 1960s Dr. Hubert Winston Smith, who ran the Law Science Academy, had bought it as a warehouse to store the furniture from the miners' homes he had purchased.

When I arrived, the "John's Store" sign was slowly fading from the fence where years earlier Mike Fisher's son Frank had once painted "George M. Spehar General Merchandise."

In the 1970s, Dr. Smith's son, Steve, remodeled the store into a pizzeria, The Saltlick, infamous for wet T-shirt contests. The next owner gutted the building while waiting in vain for town approval of six requested water tap-ins. The overhanging roof on the east, weakened by snow, was eventually deemed a public hazard, and the entire building was razed.

Betty, her sister Ann, and brothers Jake, George, Vic, and Bob grew up in a much larger town than the one today. How else to support four stores on one block?

"Society was much less mobile in those days. The norm was [that] people stayed married. The family came first. So life was really in the community," Betty explained.

"When I was little there were concrete sidewalks from Josephine and Rennie Stajduhar's house at Fifth Street and Elk Avenue up town. From Fifth Street east there was a lovely elevated platform boardwalk that connected to the passenger platform at the depot. In the evenings it was like a European paseo where folks strolled on the boardwalk and also up and down Main Street after dinner.

"There was at least one passenger car on every coal train. On Sundays we kids could hop on the car at the depot and ride it to all the sidings—up to Smith Hill Mine and Big Mine,

Josephine Stajduhar in 1984. She still lives at the corner of Fifth Street and Elk Avenue and often sat on her porch and greeted me as I went flying around the corner on my bicycle to or from my house.

     BETTY SPEHAR, GROWING UP ... NOT OLD

where they'd unhook empty cars for the next day. They'd leave them for the night shift and take the ones filled by the day shift. The real train was our play train on Sundays.

"When I had to go to the dentist, I'd hop on the train with my dad and he'd take me to the dentist in Gunnison, then I'd get to traipse along while he did a lot of business. It made me feel so grown-up."

The Spehar siblings attended school with about 400 other children. Born just one day after the cut-off date for first grade, Betty went to school anyway. Her precociousness was already showing, and there was room for her in the class.

At left is the Spehar family store on Elk Avenue in 1971, with the signs still advertising it as John's Store although it had been boarded up for years. When we arrived in 1964 it was being used as a warehouse.

One day she had her lesson finished before anyone else, so she traced a picture in her textbook while waiting. The teacher told her the principal was waiting to see her in the hall. Mortified that she had done something wrong by tracing the picture and wondering how the principal found out about it so fast, Betty left the classroom to face him.

"How'd you like to move to the second grade?" he asked. "The mine is hiring, and we'll have no room in the first grade for you." New miners meant new families and more students in the school. A relieved Betty relished the promotion.

She is convinced she had the best education possible. "There were spelling bees, and all different kinds of subjects. Grace Arnott taught music to every grade school class several times a week. We learned sight-reading, harmony, some music theory, and had a school orchestra. My instrument was the violin."

On top of that, Betty's grandparents had been tutoring her older siblings in the Croatian language a couple days a week after school. "When Bobby and I were born, we learned Croatian and English at the same time."

Betty also sang soprano and joined our small Memorial Day choir at the cemetery each year until surgery for lymphoma when she was in her seventies left her with half a larynx, reducing her once strong voice to a husky half-whisper.

"I had so many surgeries. The cure was worse than the disease. I lost my beautiful soprano. Remember when we used to sing together? Now I'm a bass," she joked with her understated droll wit. Neither age nor illness has slowed her down, however, nor altered her precise, articulate command of the language.

In the fourth grade, Betty scored so high on the standardized test that she was offered a chance to go directly to the sixth grade at the end of the year. "My parents always asked us, 'Do you *want* to?' and I decided that, yes, I did."

During her grade skipping, Betty had missed long division.

"Here I am in the sixth grade and no one approached my lack until it became obvious during 'ciphering' contests we held at school."

The contests were math competitions similar to spelling bees. The other teams, knowing Betty's weakness, always chose long division.

"Finally my pals got tired of losing and taught it to me," she recalled.

Despite Betty's straight-A report cards, her folks were not pleased when the school board hired a former football coach as superintendent. Although he had good credentials and charm, his were not the highest academic standards, and he couldn't control the children.

"We have wonderful memories of our high jinks," said Betty. "Like the time the juniors and seniors all climbed up the snowbanks over the porch canopy at the high school and entered through the second-story window."

Or the year the students dared each other to see who could go the longest without cracking a book at home.

"I went a whole year," claimed Betty.

Betty's parents offered to send her to a private academy in Canon City her senior year, but she declined, graduating at the top of her class as president and valedictorian and retaining fond memories of riding the train to Gunnison to play basketball against archrival Gunnison High School.

"We had a special train. The town band played. We snake-danced to Gunnison's new gym, and the Crested Butte teams [she was captain of the girl's team] won all the games."

A self-described tomboy, Betty credits her four brothers for her early start in all kinds of sports; softball, touch football in their large back yard, tennis—even though there were no courts—skiing, horseback riding, fishing, hiking, and sledding.

"When I was little, my brothers thought I was going to grow up and become an Olympic athlete," said Betty. They'd point to multitalented 1932 Olympian and U.S. Open Golf champion Babe Didrikson as an example for Betty to emulate.

"My brother Jake made some skis and a heel-and-toe strap for me when I was three. I had high-top boots laced to the knee. I'd ski down my sloped back yard. I learned to turn quickly or else just go into the snow bank."

After "graduating" from her back-yard slope, she skied and sledded as a youngster on "Little Hill," down Sopris from her house. Later she skied at the Pioneer Ski Area at Cement Creek, the first ski area in the state, several miles south of town.

"They were very narrow trails. You either got good or got killed," she said with a laugh.

"At one time miniature golf was the rage. I received a miniature golf course for Christmas when I was eight and set it up in the summers in the yard. I practiced putting in the living room and driving in the streets of town. Once when I was putting around the house, the ball rolled under the Christmas tree and I thought I could crawl under and retrieve it. Well, crash, it all came down with those delicate glass ornaments, just as some guests were arriving." She winced at the memory.

"I drove a golf ball through the window at the post office—luckily, not the plate glass one. And then put a window out in my dad's store. So I was banished to the back streets. Rose Sporcich was the only one of my friends who would play with me. We played who-could-get-to-the-end-of-Sopris in the fewest strokes."

Her enthusiasm was finally dampened when she accidentally hit Rose in the mouth with a club while showing her how to swing.

Summers were also for fishing in Coal Creek with a willow branch, twine, safety pin, and sinkers; potato roasts, street games, picking flowers, and helping with haying by taking lunches out to the crew.

"Our life was one glorious picnic!"

A horsewoman for seventy-five years, Betty picked up her riding skills as a young girl. Her brother Jake and his friend Rudy Malensek used to ride over Brush Creek and down into Walrod Gulch, where ten local families held regular picnics with roasted lamb and side dishes. When she was three, they put her and her sister on horses, and tied Betty on with the thongs attached to the saddle. They taught her to neck rein but stayed close in case of trouble.

"I grew up with the firm conviction from that age that I could ride anything on four legs."

She honed her skills on more cantankerous mounts.

"A herd of burros, turned loose by prospectors in the fall, subsisted on the trash in the alleys, where families put their compost heaps. When we were six or eight years old, we'd catch them, fashion a bridle with a piece of rope, and ride bareback all over the place."

The football coach/superintendent and year of no studying not withstanding, Betty excelled in academics, first at Loretto Heights in Denver and then at Rosary College in Illinois, where she earned her bachelor of arts degree. She went on to earn a master's degree and eventually a doctorate in English literature from the University of Colorado in Boulder and taught there from 1946 to 1950 and at East High School in Denver for a year.

In 1950 Betty felt a religious calling. Her devout Catholic parents had instilled in all their children a strong respect for, and love of, God. Her brother George became a priest. Oldest sister Ann was a Benedictine nun. Betty briefly entered the Cistercian order in Massachusetts. They practice contemplation, stress physical work, and observe strict silence.

"I was definitely not suited for the silence," said Betty with a smile. "I concluded that my calling was to be out in the world teaching."

She returned to Crested Butte in 1952 when the mines were closing and worked to get the mining companies to allow the miners to operate them as cooperatives.

"I wrote to all kinds of famous people and politicians enlisting their support, but all I got were a lot of autographs," she said. "I decided that if Crested Butte were going to die, I wanted to be there to hold its hand."

Rudy and Margaret Malensek at their ranch near Gunnison in 1988.
Rudy helped Betty Spehar learn to ride.

Betty hired on at the Crested Butte school.

"I taught high school English, science, Spanish, and journalism; I did the pep club, cheer-leaders, senior play, and the make-up for the junior play; and started a chapter of Quill and Scroll [a journalism honor society]. But I started getting tension headaches."

She laughed recounting how she approached the principal about her heavy load. "He said knowingly, 'I wondered how long it would take you to come in here.'"

The next year she taught junior high science and English.

"We studied the constellations with a toy planetarium in the equipment closet under the stairs by the gym, and invented a fire extinguisher in science class. There were eight or ten [students] to a class, and they were wonderful kids."

Betty recalls with particular fondness the junior high banquet.

"We had a spaghetti dinner at Frank and Gal's and then went across the street to the movies. Once a month the school personnel, from the school board members down to the janitor, had a big feast at Doc and Merree Janes' at the Elk Mountain Lodge. She'd cook din-

*Ann and Matt Malensek asked me to come to their ranch to photograph them
for their 50th wedding anniversary in 1986. Brothers Matt and Rudy married sisters
Ann and Margaret Mihelich (sisters to Tony Mihelich). After selling their ranch property
to the developers of the ski area, and later their family home on the corner of
First Street and Maroon Avenue, they moved to a ranch north of Gunnison.*

ner, and we square-danced to records. Those years were the most idyllic experience I ever had in teaching.

"In 1956 I began teaching fifty-seven varieties of English at Western State College in Gunnison," she quipped. "Everything from graduate level to freshman English."

Betty began a transitional retirement in 1982 and retired for good in 1986.

Her devotion to history and civic service made her a valuable addition to nonprofit organizations. She was one of the founders of the Crested Butte Society, Inc., in 1967 and a mover behind the restoration of the Old Rock Schoolhouse's bell tower and roof. She helped with the museum there, and again when it was reconstituted in the old railroad depot, and finally in the Spritzer building as the Crested Butte Mountain Heritage Museum before moving to its present Elk Avenue location.

One of her pet projects was tape-recording her cousin Rudy Verzuh as he reminisced about the history of the post office and real estate sales in town during the early 1950s and 1960s. Rudy was the town's first, and for many years only, realtor in addition to serving as postmaster for thirty-seven years, and owning the Princess Theatre.

"My family wants me to talk into the tape recorder and tell the family stories. I'll get to it some day," she said, and to tease me, added, "as soon as people stop calling me for interviews."

Betty explores all over the Crested Butte area in her old blue Jeep. A frequent passenger used to be Grace Arnott, her former music teacher. One of her favorite trips is seeking wild mushrooms. But the expansion of the town has frustrated her.

"It has become really distressing—seeing those huge houses turn up in the hills where we roamed so freely."

Betty's travels are not limited to the Crested Butte backcountry. During her teaching years at Western State College, she spent summers visiting countries overseas that related to her teaching courses.

"For the *Iliad* and the *Odyssey,* I traveled to Greece. For Shakespeare it was England.

"But after ten years of exploring other areas, I decided this was my favorite spot and one of the most beautiful places on earth. I have researched this point on every continent but Antarctica," she said, with a grin.

A regular at most of Crested Butte's cultural events—chamber music concerts, Mountain Theatre productions, Alpenglow concerts at the Center for the Arts, and more, Betty is a stimulating conversationalist with a deep love of people and nature.

She and I discussed politics once in the street as she returned from daily prayers at the church.

Her wry comment was, "So, President George W. Bush thinks he has a direct line to God now, does he?" She shook her head. Betty, the almost nun—if anyone has a direct line to God she'd be that person.

The elections are over now, and her "one glorious picnic of a life" is calling to her.

"There are so many things I want to do," she told me. "I never have enough time."

Rudy Verzuh, Betty's cousin, in 1987.

Esther, Rudy's wife, in 1987.

CHAPTER 18

Golden Marmots to Hollywood

The Old Town Hall, home of the Crested Butte Mountain Theatre, after a June 10th snowstorm in 1975.

H ISS AT HIM. Writhe around him. Pretend you're snakes!" encouraged Tom Towler. It was my first play, the first day of rehearsal, and he had us crawling around the floor undulating sinuously.

Tom was at the helm of an infant Crested Butte Mountain Theatre, directing men, women, and children in *Dark of the Moon.* I played one of four witches in cahoots with Eric Ross as Conjur Man taunting Vic Shepard, the Witch Boy. What we lacked in experience we made up for in enthusiasm.

Like many Crested Butte traditions, it is difficult to pinpoint the exact moment of the theater's conception. George Sibley, editor of the *Crested Butte Chronicle,* was working as a construction laborer with Tom, who had a theater background and was temporarily dropping out in Crested Butte. Match idle bar talk with creative people looking for something to sink their teeth into and . . . "Hey, let's have a community theater!" They settled it, probably over a beer: George would produce, and Tom would direct.

It seemed like the whole town got involved. As we memorized lines for the first production, friends and family helped to build the outdoor set with rough plywood and two-by-fours, scrounged no doubt by George from various construction sites. Costumes were sewn and makeup borrowed.

By August of 1972, before the nights became too cool, we four witches were in our "tree" high above the ground. With Crested Butte Mountain as our ghostly backdrop, we hissed like professionals (unpaid, of course) for the audience, who sat on blankets on the grass below.

Throughout the 1970s the Crested Butte Mountain Theatre thrived, holding performances in Mt. Crested Butte, the depot, the Gothic Building at the ski area, and the drafty Old Town Hall. After a partial remodel between 1974 and '76, and yet another in 1991, which saw the building taken off its foundation and placed on Second Street, the Old Town Hall became the CBMT permanent home. Or at least as permanent as it gets in Crested Butte.

The town of Crested Butte donated the second-floor space, and volunteers built a stage area on the north side of the room. The audience sat on tiered benches, with the first row so close that they could reach out and touch the actors' feet. Chilly in the summer and freezing in the winter, the 20-foot by 4-foot unisex backstage had mirrors along one side and blackened windows on the Elk Avenue side. The unpainted sheetrock walls were scrawled with favorite lines from plays past, and grave reminders to the cast—"Let there be no bungling!" Notes on the cluttered counter threatened death to anyone who "touches my box of hairpins." Sometimes there were nearly twenty guys and gals undressing in the same cramped room. Privacy? Who cares when you've got fifteen seconds to make a costume change.

To top it off, the building lacked an upstairs bathroom. In desperation, we invented makeshift toilet alternatives. You had your choice of the backstage pee can or the grated metal balcony suspended above Coal Creek, accessible through a backstage door. If an actor had the time or inclination, he could bypass the balcony and descend the icy, steep stairs to the street and across to the Forest Queen Hotel. The women usually opted for the pee can, the men for the balcony.

By 1980 almost every local had been involved in at least one play, and the theater attempted its first musical. *Little Mary Sunshine* was a mammoth undertaking, especially for a small town. Crested Butte houses many talented people. It's just not obvious because much of the talent is on hold while its owner is washing dishes at night and working in a ski rental shop during the day to make ends meet.

The musical was "directed" by an electronics expert who, as far as could be determined, had minimal theater experience. Mostly he just told people where to move on stage. He couldn't even sing.

Almost no one had professional training. Walking and talking at the same time was tricky for the guys. And the nuances of dialogue escaped them, especially some of the flowery phrases of *Little Mary Sunshine,* set in the early 1900s. Most of the men were athletic, and all were skiers. Why else would they be in Crested Butte? But teaching these "athletes" to march in step and sing at the same time took the full two months of rehearsal. Singing was my forte, but I wasn't skilled enough for the goody-two-shoes title role, and was chosen for the supporting part of her feisty sidekick, Nancy Twinkle. The cast threatened mutiny about two weeks before opening night, citing such problems as lack of direction, and drunkenness on the part of the director and many of the male cast members. The only upside of the entire production was that in our long, dressy period costumes no one could see we were on the pee can.

Many productions later I realized that two weeks before opening, chaos always reigns. No one knows his lines. The set is unfinished; wood, sawdust, and tools are scattered all over the stage when the actors need to rehearse; and we all have a single thought: what the heck am I doing here? The answer, of course: applause.

In 1981 the CBMT board decided to applaud in a more tangible way the casts, directors, and backstage people who contributed all their waking hours to entertaining the town.

"Something like the Academy Awards, only Crested Butte style," suggested the theater board president.

Jokester Eric Ross cackled, "Let's call it the Golden Marmots!" A Colorado rodent sometimes referred to as a "whistle pig," marmots are abundant around Crested Butte.

That year there were Golden Marmot awards for "Best Supporting Actor and Actress," "Best in a Lead Role," "Best Director," and so on. With typical Crested Butte goofiness, an award was also given to Rae Lyn Jacobs's huge sheepdog. Back then everyone brought his or her dog to rehearsal to avoid the dogcatcher or keeping the animal for long hours on a chain. Unlike Denis Hall's black lab, Scratch, who jumped on stage any time an actor raised his voice at Denis in rehearsal, Rae Lyn's dog snored patiently while Rae Lyn cried, screamed,

Eric Ross and Morgan Queal in 1983 in The Good Doctor.

and was dragged around stage by the villain, earning him the "Best Dog" award.

Eric Ross and Patricia Dawson shared a "What's My Line?" award. Both great actors, they were notorious for forgetting their lines. Pat clutched her script like a baby grabs its "blanky" until the very last moment. According to fellow cast members, she penciled in cue lines on the wall of the *Ladyhouse Blues* set. Everyone in *Equus* memorized both their own lines and Eric's. There was no telling where he would jump into the scene. The fact that Eric directed *Equus* as well as portrayed the psychiatrist in the leading role made it that much more difficult for him. I don't have too many complaints. I won my first Marmot for "Best Supporting Actress" for my portrayal of Dora, the mother in *Equus*. It was an unwelcome portent of roles to come.

Possibly the most imaginative feature of the awards ceremony was the design of the Marmots themselves.

"I borrowed a mold from the Western State College art department," Eric recalled. "We cast the marmots in plaster of Paris and spray-painted them gold. Only they didn't quite have time to dry right," he told me sheepishly. Twenty years later, when I dust the items on my desk and move the Marmot, the paint rubs off on my hands.

Eric admitted to bribing some kids the following year to cast molds of a squirrelly-looking rodent six inches tall, holding a nut in its front paws, and paint them "harvest gold." More yellow than glittery golden, the paint at least stayed on the rodents. But again the plaster didn't dry properly, and many Marmot winners found their prize crumbling in their hands. The Marmot master of ceremonies loved to tease Eric while holding up the dusty, yellow remains of his 1982 Marmot in a plastic bag.

"Here folks, this is what your Marmot will look like in a couple of months, so handle it carefully."

By the third year, the winners took home a heavy, gold statuette ordered from a trophy company. Real official looking, it had a faux marble base. No more plaster of Paris whistle pigs. We had gone bigtime. The "Best Director" award winner gave a short acceptance speech ending with, "Isn't it wonderful how the Marmot statuettes have improved over the years?" He raised it over his head in victory, and the base fell off.

An array of Golden Marmot statuettes, displayed by a masked Kathleen Mary in 1985.

Perusing the trophy catalog years later, I discovered that those gold awards, looking suspiciously like rabbits, are actually chinchillas. Golden Chinchilla Awards … no, just doesn't have the right ring to it.

MUSICALS ARE ALWAYS POPULAR with audiences but are a pain in the neck to produce. Kathleen Mary—another non-musician—(who missed the *Little Mary Sunshine* fiasco) was obsessed with *Cabaret*. It was a mammoth undertaking in terms of cast size, period costumes, set changes, and, as always, money. We were so poor we sometimes had to rent scripts and musical scores. But she convinced the theater board to let her stage it in 1985.

This time, at least, the cast was more talented, led by former professional dancer Heidi Coe Duval, who whipped the sexy dancers into shape and was persuaded to take the lead. Michael Danna with his soaring, trained tenor portrayed the Master of Ceremonies. I auditioned for the role of the alluring chanteuse (played by Lisa Minnelli in the movie version) before it was offered to Heidi. To my dismay I was cast as the sixtyish widow Fraulein Schneider. I had to grey my hair, paint wrinkles on my face and wear dowdy clothes and clunky shoes. I was only thirty-six years old at the time, so I felt it was a pretty big stretch. Plus my "love interest" was my father's age.

Since this was my third old lady role, preceded by *Equus* and *The Children's Hour,* I was beginning to wonder if I was being typecast. My Golden Marmot for "Best Supporting Actress" in *Cabaret* more than made up for it.

Cabaret's biggest hurdle was the set. The director insisted on a realistic walled set full of Victorian (all borrowed, all fragile) furniture. And it had to be reversible: when you turned each of the four walls (flats) around, there was a totally different set complete with furniture and props. Every cast member was assigned to a flat. The strong guys pushed the walls around; the rest of us ran in with furniture and props. During the first dress rehearsal the set change took ninety minutes. We got it down to two minutes by opening night.

Cabaret was the first CBMT production to feature a live band. Make that a live band in drag. The script called for a four-girl band. We could only come up with two female musicians, so the two men dolled up as women complete with wigs, falsies, tight dresses, lipstick, and mascara. The flautist was a well-built bicycle racer, ski coach, and rather shy guy with thinning hair—a closet hunk. He was lovely as a platinum blonde in a stylish 1930s hat, if you overlooked the neatly trimmed beard and mustache.

Heidi Duval, in white, with the Cabaret *dance-hall girls, 1985.*

Following one performance, as the rest of us were changing back into street clothes, he methodically exchanged his demure, black dress costume for a bright red frock and pulled on fishnet stockings, size Huge, over his muscular quads. He carefully applied more makeup (having shaved the night before), including fake eyelashes and bright red lipstick, then completed the ensemble with a tasteful strand of white pearls.

"Don, are you crazy?" asked a member of the puzzled cast. "You're supposed to be taking the makeup off, not putting it on."

"I'm off to the Grubstake to compete in the Red Lady Ball contest. I have to admit I had a difficult time at the thrift shop in Grand Junction finding a dress the right size. But don't you think this one looks all right?"

Damned if he wasn't the runner-up Red Lady, cheered on by an enthusiastic *Cabaret* cast.

Theater makeup was almost as challenging as learning lines. Most mountain women don't wear makeup like city

Master of Ceremonies Michael Danna in Cabaret, *flanked by two dancers.*

folk do. It was a shock to slather on foundation, eyeliner, fake eyelashes, powder, blush, and lipstick, not to mention drawing in the wrinkle lines for old people, which after my three "mature woman" roles I had mastered. The guys, who could wield a pool cue with uncanny accuracy, couldn't even begin to touch their eyelashes with the end of the mascara wand. Hand-to-eye coordination reverted to that of a three-year-old, as did attitudes.

"No way I'm putting on lipstick," whined one. "Are you sure I need this mascara? How do you keep your hand still and not poke out your eye?"

Back stage was crazy— ringing with cries of "pass the blush. Where's the Kleenex? We're out of tissues. Use this roll of toilet paper. Has anyone seen my—?"

Linda Wilson, makeup expert, moved up and down the counter fixing faces and periodically crying out in frustration, "Now put everything back and keep it clean!"

"Where is back?" retorted a smart aleck.

A twenty-person cast can't put it back, because everything just keeps getting passed around the room. And no matter how careful we were, a fine dusting of powder always

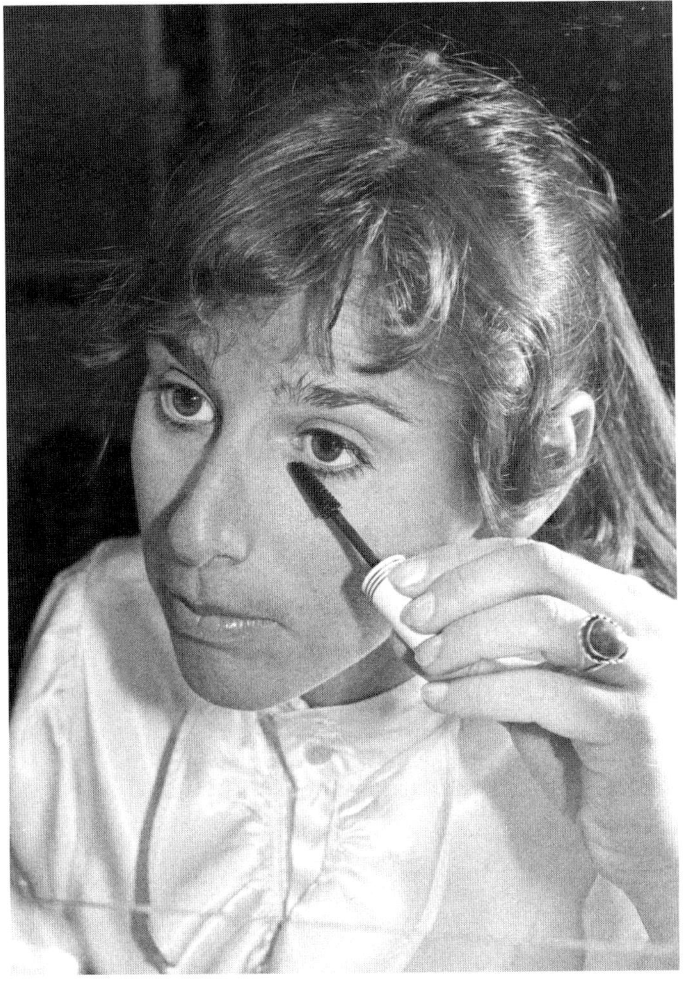

Cindy Petito in 1985, a multiple Marmot winner,
got the mascara application skill down pat.

coated the counter, our street clothes, and costumes.

When Tom Towler left Crested Butte, Eric Ross, who had performed with Second City in Chicago, took up the reins. A master at improvisation and persuasion, Eric could get anyone to do anything. For about two days before auditions, he beat the streets cajoling, flattering, and demanding. That way, between the old hands, street recruits, and naive auditioners, who had no idea they were turning the next three months of their lives over to Eric, he would be sure to find enough actors.

Here's how he got me in 1982 for *Whose Life Is It, Anyway?*

"Sandy, I've got this great part for you." Flashing a coy smile, he poked his curly head into the Paragon Gallery, where I was working.

"Yeah?" No longer a naive auditioner, I was immediately skeptical.

"All you have to do is play a quadriplegic and lay around a couple of hours. No costume but a hospital gown, no stage movements to memorize." And then the ultimate temptation: "Hardly any makeup. You've got to look sick."

"Can I win a Golden Marmot for Best Lead Actress?"

"Absolutely."

I was hooked. After that, Eric persuaded me to lie in that hospital bed, hooked up to a fake IV, not just during the show but a half-hour prior to curtain time and all during the twenty-minute intermission. I was supposed to be sleeping, but I loved cracking one eye open to watch the audience's reaction when they passed by the stage on the way to their seats.

I missed the backstage camaraderie, though. I missed being warm even more. The bed covers were as skimpy as the tie-in-the-back hospital gown, and Eric neglected to turn on the heat until showtime. I lay there in character unable to move, lest I break the spell Eric was trying to weave. But by intermission, I had started to shiver, and I had to clamp my jaws to keep my teeth from chattering too loudly.

"Hey, someone better go out there and make sure Cortner doesn't have hypothermia," came a whisper from the wings. My nurse in the show was the logical choice. He pretended to adjust the IV and rubbed my hands, trying to warm me, staying in character the whole time.

"Billy, could you bring me a blanket?" I whispered. And, I thought desperately, jump in here and warm me up.

I think Eric took perverse pleasure in watching me helped out of bed by two cast members so I could take a bow at the end. My circulation was so slow after three motionless hours that I could hardly walk.

But I won that "Lead Actress" Marmot, just as he had promised.

IN THE EARLY 1980s Crested Butte Mountain Theatre went semi-professional, hiring former resident Barbara Fitzsimmons Segal to direct a Shakespeare production each summer. Those plays had "casts of thousands" and were traditionally done outdoors or in a large tent rented for the occasion. It always rained or was freezing cold for the rehearsals and performances. For several years, the unheated metal, former county road-maintenance building next to the softball field (remodeled in 1987 into the Center for the Arts) served as a makeup/dressing room. "Backstage" was the inside of a Mountain Express bus parked behind the tent.

Don "Tuck" Tucker was a tall ageless guy who could kiss my hand and grab my butt in the same move as I boarded his Mountain Express bus. He rode his black horse in the summer and was always courting one lady or another. His commanding voice earned him a role as *Othello,* and several Golden Marmots.

During *Romeo and Juliet,* Tuck was "killed" in a sword fight in the first act. My character committed suicide shortly after, and when the act was over I hiked up my costume skirt and petticoats and crossed the street to hang out at home until the curtain call. One night in the backstage bus Tuck and I made a pact.

"Man, I hate losing all my summer nights for this," he complained. I never get to ride my horse. And I miss _________ (fill in the name of his lady of the season)."

I agreed. "I'm sick of being inside while everyone else is playing softball."

"Here we are freezing our behinds rehearsing in this tent all night, *every* night, and we gotta die in Act 1."

"I wouldn't mind it quite so much if we didn't have to come back for the curtain call two acts later," I pointed out.

"OK, let's make a pact. No more summer plays," he proposed.

"Absolutely, winter plays only!"

We shook hands on it.

The next spring as I hopped onto Tuck's bus to go skiing we discussed the casting call for the big summer production.

"Are you auditioning? I hear it's a great part," I asked.

Tom Mallardi in A Midsummer Night's Dream *in 1992.*

"No, how 'bout you?"

"Nope." And we shook hands again.

I was the first to break the pact two summers later, in 1987, when the board of directors hired professional director James Bohnen from Denver. James tried to cast a Shakespeare play. Not enough men. Guess Tuck and I weren't the only ones to make a pact. So he chose *To Gillian on Her 37th Birthday* and guided our small cast to a Marmot for "Best Play." It was one of the first plays to hit the stage of the new Center for the Arts.

I auditioned because I was dying to see how it was to work under a professionally trained director. It was all I had dreamed of. He was so organized that we only had to rehearse about three times a week, as opposed to every night. Plus the center had two—count 'em, two—dressing rooms, one for guys and one for the girls, and two inside toilets!

James Bohnen's reputation grew each year, and he chose plays with large casts so that he could include as many community members as possible. One was *Our Town,* in 1989, wherein Marcie Telander pantomimed shelling peas so skillfully, I could see and hear them clink into the bowl. *The Man Who Came to Dinner* featured Tom Mallardi, who roared to a Golden Marmot as the man who walked to dinner, overstayed his welcome, and left in a wheelchair. Cindy Petito's prim Nurse Preen stole the show—and another Golden Marmot. I played the mother, Mrs. Stanley. An old lady, *again.*

James gently broke the news to me one evening over drinks: "Sandy, you are no longer an ingenue."

"You mean, I'm stuck playing an old lady forever?

"Well . . ." he hedged. But I got it.

Great, I'd spent my younger years portraying old ladies. And after hitting forty, I'm old hat myself, although I did manage to win a "Leading Actress Role" Marmot in 1993 for my final musical, as Kate in *Kiss Me, Kate.* But that was because I could sing.

It's different for guys. Much like a Hollywood counterpart, Tom Mallardi started his CBMT career portraying dashing young Shakespearean heroes. As he gained more weight and his beard grayed, he excelled in patriarch roles. Comedy, tragedy, irony, you name it, Tom could do it, and won every Marmot there was to win. After his death in 2002 the upstairs of the Old Town Hall was christened the Thomas A. Mallardi Cabaret Theatre in his honor.

Some of our fellow thespians even made the Big Time: I saw Tom Towler's name in the credits of some television shows. John McCormack, the narrator for *Our Town,* moved to Hollywood, hired an agent, and was last seen in commercials, minor television roles (including a gig on *Star Trek*), and major motion pictures.

Thousands of people have contributed their love, dedication, money, talent, and time to the Crested Butte Mountain Theatre since 1972, and it has become one of the oldest community theaters in the state. If Tom Towler could only see us now!

At the gala opening of the new Center for the Arts in December 1987, Heidi Coe Duval choreographed a dance to music from the "Nutcracker Suite" and titled it "Dance of the Sugar Plum Fairies." It brought down the house. Starring, from left, Bill Crank, Crested Butte town manager; Thom Cox, Crested Butte State Bank president; John Norton, vice president of marketing at the ski area; and "Du" Duval, Heidi's good-natured ski patrolman husband.

CHAPTER 19

Grace Arnott

Grace Arnott in 1988.

GRACE ARNOTT WAS EVERYTHING her name implied: graceful, elegant, gentle, and soft-spoken.

My sister met her before I did.

"I first remember seeing her in her garden," recalled Kathleen. "She was wearing a green robe and a wide-brimmed straw hat with a green ribbon tied under her chin. After we got to know each other, we would visit in the garden. She must have been close to eighty then."

"What do you know about Craig Hall? He lives next door to me," Grace inquired of her one day.

Kathleen and Craig were old friends. But before she could tell Grace that, she answered her own question.

"He does his laundry and hangs his sheets on the clothesline, so he must be a nice person," she concluded. Then she confided to Kathleen, "If you sleep alone you only have to wash your sheets every other week instead of once a week."

There was something respectable in Crested Butte about hanging out your laundry, especially sheets.

I officially met Grace when Kathleen sent me across their alley one day to a little white house with red trim next to the Union Congregational Church.

I knocked tentatively on the side door.

"Hi, I'm Kathleen's sister. She said maybe you would be willing to let me pick some of your rhubarb."

"I don't know why not. Here, let me show you where it is." She put the straw hat on her snowy hair and tied the green ribbon before descending the steps with her cane. Slowly she led me toward the alley where several enormous rhubarb plants grew in the shade of her shed.

"Here are the plants," she said, and gestured with her delicate, expressive hand. "Just pick all you want, dear. They grow like weeds. But be sure to leave enough for Gayle [my sister's roommate]. She'll be wanting some for the pie she's baking."

Years later, in 1988, when I was privileged to interview Grace for a local publication she generously shared stories from her life.

Grace wasn't born in Crested Butte, even though many of us considered her an "old-timer." She arrived as a young lady in the fall of 1927 from her Everest, Kansas, hometown.

"I had never seen such flowing streams and towering peaks. And the aspens were turning and were such beautiful colors of gold," she marveled. "I fell in love with it, and I've been in love ever since."

Born August 7, 1900, Grace Curran was the youngest of eleven children.

"I love to sing, but I was too much of an introvert to do anything with my voice. And although I play some piano, I didn't have the hands for it. I've always wanted to be a teacher," she told me. Her teaching career started early. Her first-grade teacher asked her to tutor classmates having trouble reading. Grace herself was taught "to read and do numbers by my older sisters before I started school."

"When I was young, it was possible to teach right out of high school. So at seventeen, I drove a horse and buggy to teach at a country school for $50 a month."

"What about college?" I asked.

"It took me five years of summer school, but I finally graduated from Emporia State Teachers College in Kansas and took a teaching job in Hayden, Arizona. It was a copper-mining company town, and they paid me $500 a year plus travel expenses to Kansas."

"That must be why you finally came to Crested Butte, to get away from the heat," I said. I grew up in Arizona. The summer heat was stifling.

"No," she corrected me firmly. "I had been offered three jobs. But this one paid the most: $1,600 a year. So naturally I accepted it. I conducted the girls and boys glee clubs and mixed choir and directed the whole school Christmas program."

When the lovely blue-eyed, twenty-seven-year-old petite redhead, who wore her braids wound around her head, arrived in Crested Butte, there were five working coal mines. The Big Mine was open seven days a week, around the clock, and a boardwalk extended uptown from the railroad depot at the eastern end of Elk Avenue.

The old train depot at the end of Elk Avenue in 1983.

"I first roomed at Ritter's, on Elk Avenue in the home Martha and Whitey Sporcich now own, and since there were no restaurants, the Ritters invited me for dinner. Later Mrs. Hartman, who lived in this house, which we eventually purchased, took me in as a boarder for a dollar a day, which included three meals."

A flu epidemic swept Crested Butte during Christmas 1928, which delayed the reopening of the school. James Arnott's wife was one of those who died, leaving him with four children to raise. James was the outside foreman and master mechanic at the Peanut Mine. Grace had met him previously at one of the community dances. Later they began to court.

"He was a beautiful dancer. He had taken dancing lessons from Charlie Ross, owner of the Peanut Mine. We had dances every Saturday night at the Elk Mountain House (now Donita's), Mattivi's (Frank and Gal's), or the Old Town Hall. You didn't have to have a date. You could eat luscious ham sandwiches downstairs at the Old Town Hall and dance upstairs. After one dance, he took me over to the drugstore (in the Grubstake Building) to have a sandwich, and then he walked me home."

A five-year courtship ensued, highlighted by their dancing dates. Grace finally married the six-foot, two-inches-tall James Arnott in Salida on June 7, 1933. They lived for a while in a mining company house owned by the Colorado Fuel and Iron Company near the Elk Mountain Lodge. James's four older children were soon joined by two with Grace: son Jim and daughter Mary Helen. Several years later they purchased the house on Maroon—six children took up a lot of space.

It wasn't until 1943 that Grace returned to teaching, only because so many high school teachers were overseas fighting in the war. It didn't take long for the school superintendent to discover her talents.

"I taught geometry, algebra, English, spelling, reading, Latin, and history. I had to study ahead on some of those subjects because I was learning along with the students," she said, smiling at the memory. "My specialty, of course, was music."

After the mines closed in 1952, she spent two years teaching in Trinidad, Colorado. The lower elevation gave James some relief; years of breathing coal dust had taken their toll. He died in December 1957, the same year as his mother, from "black lung"—emphysema.

Grace recalled, "It was a hard year for me, losing two of my loved ones at the same time."

She returned to teaching in Crested Butte, and by the time she retired, generations of Crested Butte natives had been her students, including Marilyn Rozman, Trudy Yaklich, John Somrak, Lyle and Mildred McNeill, Martha and Whitey Sporcich, Jim Somrak, Rudy Sedmak, Betty Spehar, and Willard Ruggera, just to name several. They all still called her "Mrs. Arnott."

Grace never had disciplinary problems with her pupils. In those days, she recalled, "Teachers were thought of as someone special, to be esteemed."

One former student remembered, "All she had to do was look at you and you toed the line. When I was a fourth grader she put the fear of God in me, and I can tell you one thing for sure—I still wouldn't talk back to her."

 GRACE ARNOTT

The Old Rock Schoolhouse, in 1984, where Grace taught school in 1927.

Others insisted she didn't have a mean bone in her body, yet commanded utmost respect.

Grace recalled a Cowbelles' essay contest in which Marilyn Rozman (then Marilyn Probst) and Trudy Yaklich took first and second place respectively on "Ways to Use Beef."

"We were always winning contests," she said proudly.

Since her retirement, she lived alone in the little white house. When winters got to be too hard, Grace started splitting them between her son Jim in Pennsylvania and daughter Mary Helen Guardipee in Virginia, with other visits to her four stepchildren. That's resulted in a great deal of traveling, something Grace enjoyed mightily.

"Jim is with the Forest Service, and Mary Helen married a park ranger. I've been to the Grand Canyon, Everglades, Key Largo, Chincoteague Island, and countless national parks. But as soon as the snow melts, I return home to Crested Butte and this white house that enfolds me as soon as I walk into it," she said.

"Long before I knew you, I photographed your house," I told her. "I love the symmetry of it."

"Well," she replied tartly, "I do have some trouble getting the churchgoers to remember not to park in front of my driveway."

In addition to keeping up with news of her own grandchildren and great-grandchildren, she became a surrogate grandmother to Gracie, the first child of my sister's roommate Gayle and her husband, Bob Bernard.

"I mowed Grace's lawn, cleaned her house, or took her to have her hair styled. I loved to listen to her talk about the old days," Gayle Bernard told me.

Grace had definite opinions about students being bused from Crested Butte to Gunnison after the high school closed in 1966. The last graduating class had only four members. By comparison, right before the mines closed she was teaching about thirty-five children per class.

"Sending students on a bus and wasting so much of their day is bad. But so is only having two people in a class. There is no competition," she said.

One day she discussed with me her thoughts on the growth of Crested Butte.

"I wouldn't like to see the town get too large. The development of Crested Butte is getting out of hand. I miss the old days and the old people that used to live here."

There was a wistful tone to her voice. She had outlived many of her contemporaries and even her students. She still never locked her door.

"It's sad that people have a tendency to make this place over into what they came from."

Not your typical retiree, Grace was sharp as a tack, feisty, and a master of detail. She joined in life with relish, as a football fan, attending potlucks at the Senior Citizens Center, walking around town, going to church, and dining out. One friend told me how she corrected his professional papers, sometimes bringing out her *McGuffey's Reader* to make a point.

Grace attributed her longevity to "the grace of God. He has been good to me," she often said. Every Sunday she sat on the right-hand side of the third row at the Queen of All Saints Catholic Church, arriving early to pray alone. Weeks before her death she was still making the two and one-half block walk to church, an indication of how good she felt. Although she had a hip replacement and had lost her kneecap in an automobile accident, Grace remained healthy until the day she died. She walked slowly and carefully. The first time I put out a hand to steady her, she tactfully chided me.

       GRACE ARNOTT

Tom Arnott, Grace's brother-in-law, in 1982. A quiet man, he often walked out to Peanut Lake, shouldering his rifle, because "you never know if you're going to get into a skunk or bear."

"I really wish people wouldn't try to take my arm to help me up stairs and curbs. I know you have good intentions and want to help me," she explained, "but it's more likely you might upset my balance and actually hinder me, not aid me."

I apologized, and felt her delicate fingers squeeze my hand.

She was surprised and delighted by a party on her ninety-second birthday in 1992. Her friends Nick Rayder and Tom Duncanson blew up ninety-two helium balloons in her honor and held a joint birthday dinner at the Slogar Restaurant with the Reverend Jim Koenigsfeld, who was celebrating his fiftieth birthday the same day. Two weeks later, she was felled by a stroke; she died Monday, August 24, 1992.

She left behind a town whose changes had saddened her. But she would have been thrilled to see the high school finally return to Crested Butte in 1996. Trudy Yaklich, the young essay contest winner, took Grace's lessons to heart and dedicated her own teaching career to helping Mexican children in Arizona learn to speak English—a tribute to Grace's skill and love.

James' brother, Hank Arnott, in 1969 at Frank and Gal's.

Since her death, Grace's house has remained vacant, unchanged in the sea of remodeled homes around it. Semi-sheer white curtains cloak its windows. The churchgoers still block the driveway, overgrown with grass, even though the rest of the lawn is mowed regularly. And, crouching next to the shed, I take "all you want, dear," cherishing the memory of her carefully descending the back steps, cane in hand, white hair covered by her straw hat.

CHAPTER 20

Vinotok 1988:
The Fall Wine Festival

John Somrak, one of the Vinotok founders, found a 100-year-old Indian Head penny in his back yard in 1980. He squeezed me in a bear hug before proudly displaying his treasure for my camera.

EATING, DRINKING, DANCING, and storytelling—that was the essence of the first Vinotok, dreamed up in 1985 by Marcie Telander with old-timers Frank Orazem, John and Frances Somrak, and other members of the Two Buttes Senior Citizens Center.

These elders told Marcie about Crested Butte's earliest days, when their Eastern European forebears celebrated the finishing of last year's homemade wine and the laying down of the new wine. Italians, Slavs, and Germans competed for the best homemade wines. The literal translation in Croatian of the word *vinotok* is "fall wine festival." In Germany and Austria it coincides with the autumn equinox and is known as Oktoberfest. This big blowout is centuries old and has many variations. Regardless, bringing in the last of the harvest before winter offers a good excuse for a down-home celebration.

Crested Butte's modern version of the wine festival draws heavily from legendary medieval figures. Representing the bounty of the season, the Harvest Mother is portrayed by a visibly pregnant lady. The Green Man symbolizes the virility and fertility of the earth. The Dragon stands for nature and all its wonders, and Sir Hapless refers to modern technology and manufactured items. Dancers represent the changing of the seasons.

The Great Grump (I'm not sure of its origin, but the name is classic Crested Butte) is a manifestation of what I call "out with the old and in with the new." Residents write their personal grumps and gripes on a slip of paper and toss it into the "Grump Box" at the post office. Later the contents of the boxes are emptied into the hollow interior of the Great Grump, a part human, part animal-like form similar to a huge Mexican piñata.

The weeklong mid-September Vinotok also incorporated a storytelling celebration during the first few years. Each night was host to a different style—ghost stories, children's stories, stories told by professional storytellers, and a Liar's Contest in a local bar, wherein contestants might grease their tongues before launching their straight-faced lies. The finale came Saturday night. Marcie Telander, queen of the storytellers, persuaded many a shy old-timer to ascend the stage at the Mountain Theatre in the Old Town Hall and regale us with tales of "way back when." John Somrak made his debut using eight pages of handwritten notes on a yel-

Marcie Telander encourages the storytellers in 1990 by telling one of her own.

low legal pad to relate the history of Crested Butte. The second year he was funnier and less long-winded, but he never got over being nervous. The old-timers told true stories from the heart, and the audience was honored by their personal revelations.

After the storytelling we all assembled outside for the raucous Vinotok parade led down Elk Avenue to Sixth Street by the Harvest Mother, Green Man, and various medieval performers, mummers, and torch bearers. Along the way the characters stopped in at local bars for a bit of refueling.

At the four-way-stop parking lot, a duel between the Dragon and Sir Hapless culminated in a trial in which the Great Grump was found guilty (of what, I never could quite figure out) and sentenced to burn at the stake—in reality a giant bonfire.

That's where things really heated up. A fire in Crested Butte, particularly during a slow time of year, is bound to draw just about everyone in town. It was reminiscent of a Middle Ages witch burning. We danced around the flames, chanting "Burn the Grump! Burn the Grump!" Because the fire was less than a block from my house, I saw the smoke and flames rising high above the Alpineer Building and drawn like a moth, ran over to shoot photos, shielding my camera from the intense heat that forced the circle of people further and fur-

The Green Man, Scott Wimmer, husband of Glo Cunningham, the Earth Mother,
dances around the bonfire in 1989.

ther from the fire. The Great Grump with his belly full of nasty thoughts was torched. We cheered and cheered, and the circle danced faster and faster around the inferno.

Even though as a reporter and photographer for the newspaper I was obligated to report on all the Vinotok activities, the traditional pochenka—the Slovenian lamb roast—was closest to my heart; the polka party afterwards came in a close second. All that legend stuff was just a prelude to the highlight of the week.

The Vinotok pochenka, steeped in Old World tradition, reflected the melting-pot culture of the Serbs, Croats, Germans, English, and Irish who settled the town in the 1800s. In its reincarnation it was designed as a community potluck. Residents brought their traditional specialties, and the Vinotok committee provided the main course: the lamb.

I'll take a leg of lamb, medium rare, over a filet mignon any day. Couple the lamb with local treats such as Leola Yaklich's melt-in-your-mouth povitica, Botsie Spritzer's homemade klobassi sausage, and Mildred McNeill's light, tender biscuits, just to name a few— well, you can imagine. I'm hungry just writing about it.

Sid Niccoli and his son Bobby hosted the first Vinotok pochenka in 1986 at their ranch down valley. Bobby contributed the two lambs, and Sid designed an electric spit turner. The men and their friends stayed up all night sipping Old Weller and Wild Turkey and trading stories.

In 1988, Joyce and John Cobai roasted one lamb at the Town Park, and I decided to hang out with them for a while to see how it was done.

Traditionally the preparation of the roast is strictly a male activity, beginning with the slaughter of the lamb (in some families it's a goat, and no, I wasn't there for that part) right down to the carving of the roast. Of course we know which sex cleans up after it all.

I eyeballed the lamb doubtfully.

"Joyce, do you really think one lamb is enough? There are going to be some hungry folks down at the Senior Center. Even though it's a potluck, you

Mary Yaklich with her mother, Leola Yaklich, who is slicing her home-made povitica at a family reunion in 1980.

know the lamb is the star of the show." I calculated there could be up to 150 people waiting to feast.

Her assured answer: "Don't be silly, there's always enough. Last year we roasted three lambs, and we were begging people to take leftovers."

Where was I, out of town?

John and Joyce explained their technique while we waited for the lamb to complete its twelve-hour journey to succulent tenderness.

"Garlic is the key," they agreed. "I cut holes just under the fatty skin and insert cloves of garlic," explained John. "And then it's real important to tie the lamb on the spit with its legs tightly trussed with wire."

Added Joyce, "Here's why: the meat shrinks during the roasting. One year the lamb fell off the spit. Oh, it was a real mess! We just had to grab it out of the fire and tie it back on and cook it some more." She rolled her eyes at the memory. Once the lamb was prepared, Johnny checked out the wood for the fire. "You can only use aspen wood. If you burn any other kind, such as cedar or apple, the lamb takes on the taste of the wood."

The wood fires were built on each side of the spit, not directly underneath. This allowed the meat to heat evenly as the spit turned. The spit was suspended about two feet above the fires, which must be slow-burning and not too hot to insure the tenderness of the roast.

"Last year the meat cooked too fast. It wasn't as tender as it should have been," said Joyce. A woman after my own heart, that Joyce. Nothing worse than tough lamb.

Johnny shook the seasoning salt onto the roast. As soon as the juices started dripping into the fire, he salted it one last time. "During the day," he said, "I baste it with butter."

Joyce took the first shift turning the spit. The handle was rigged with a bicycle chain and gears to make the job easier—like pedaling a bike, but with your hands instead of your feet. Because the park lacked electricity, Sid Niccoli's invention wouldn't have been much good today.

After Joyce tired of turning the spit, daughter Melina took a try, and as I dropped in and out during the day to check on their progress, I saw John's sister Darlene Halazon and her husband, Fred, sharing shifts, as well as Scott Sylvester, who had helped design the bicycle-chain handle.

Anyone who wandered down to the park was graciously invited to help. It was a hot and tedious job. By the end of the day, pieces of roofing tin had been placed around the end of the spit, shielding the turner from the heat.

The procedure had begun at five on a cold, mitten-wearing morning. But by five p.m., when the meat was taken off the spit, everyone was stripped down to shorts and T-shirts.

All day we just hung around, gossiped a little, drank a beer or two, and enjoyed an Indian Summer afternoon, the scent of lamb bathing us with the promise of the feast to come.

Finally Johnny stuck a knife into the lamb's breast, pulled it out, then quickly licked his finger and dabbed it onto the blade, where a brief sizzle was heard.

"If the tip is hot when you pull it out, it's done," he explained. And so it was, according to Johnny's finger.

John Cobai and Johnny Leverett take a turn on the spit in 1987, when three lambs were roasted.

He and Fred Halazon lifted the spit with its precious cargo onto the picnic table, which had been covered with a clean oilcloth and a large cutting board. Each wielding a long, razor-sharp knife, they began to cut the lamb into pieces. Long hot hours on the spit had been rewarded. The tender meat dropped from the bones at the gentlest touch of the blade.

Joyce took a sample and popped it into her mouth. "Well, I don't know." She chewed thoughtfully. "It could be a *little* more tender." And she grabbed a tidbit from a different part of the lamb, just to check. I admired her self-control.

She nodded her approval, and big chunks of lamb hit the pans. Scraps of meat on the carving board were cleaned up, fingers licked, lips smacking; a faint murmur of pleasure rippled through us.

"A chance to pick privately," said Marcie Telander. She, like me, is an insatiable lamb lover.

Joyce, Darlene, Marcie, and the other lucky ladies who had gotten a much-coveted preview covered the big pans with foil for transport to the Senior Center on Elk Avenue. The community potluck side dishes were already on the buffet table. Picnic tables on the street with their red-checkered tablecloths awaited the feasters, and the polka band warmed up under the overhang of the Senior Center.

All of those who had begged off spit duty arrived at the park. Some hoped for a private pick on the way up town.

"Here, I'll take a pan in my car."

We pitied those waiting for the popular main entrée while we were taking a nibble here and there at the park. Our preview merely whetted our appetites.

"Don't worry," Joyce said again. "There's going to be enough for everyone." She shooed us all up to the center with our lamb pans.

But by the time the Cobais cleaned up and drove to the feast, all the lamb had been consumed and the volunteers in the kitchen were gnawing at the bones. The empty side dishes testified to the size of the crowd.

"It's okay," said Joyce. "We got enough to eat while we were carving, didn't we, Johnny." It was a statement, not a question. Johnny, more taciturn than usual, nodded briefly. Joyce was immediately bubbling with ideas for next year.

"Let's go over to Paonia the day before the pochenka and pick one up there. It's cheaper, and they'll butcher it for us."

That day's lamb had been purchased during the Gunnison Cattlemen's Days 4-H sale. For several years a longtime local ranching family had donated a lamb, but they no longer raised sheep.

"An all-town party is an expensive proposition," said Marcie. "We don't have a lot of money in the checkbook. Anyone who brought a side dish paid only $2 to cover expenses. Because it's a community festival, we count on a lot of people contributing in different ways. Otherwise it might not happen."

And after a while, it didn't. Over the years, many of the old-timers involved had died or moved away to lower, warmer climes. Although the remaining families often held their own lamb roasts, the pochenka was discontinued in the early 1990s, several years after Johnny Cobai's death. And also because, as Marcie puts it, "It was very energy- and time-consuming, and each year we were feeding more and more people, with fewer Crested Butte originals who knew the recipes and pochenka process." She stepped down as the head of Vinotok in 1993, although she has kept a hand in over the ensuing years, passing on the legends to new directors.

Since the wonderful lamb years, Vinotok has changed. Younger people these days seem to be more focused on the parade and the burning of the Great Grump. The bonfire at the four-way-stop finally got so out of hand that fire engines were stationed there to keep the surrounding buildings from catching fire. Hotheaded college kids, ignorant of the Vinotok traditions, were throwing in skis and computers. The Fire Department banned the giant blaze in 2003. The parade went west that year on Elk Avenue instead of east. And the Great Grump was burned over a cauldron, a la Harry Potter.

Marcie and I reminisce occasionally, lamenting the lost lamb roast. I've been to other private parties with roasted lamb but have never seen the lamb slow-cooked like it was during Vinotok. Yet the smoky smell transports me back to the pochenka on an Indian Summer day, and I can hear Joyce in the back of my mind, saying, "It could be just a *little* more tender . . ."

Botsie Spritzer made klobassi sausage on his kitchen table with an antique sausage maker and hung it in his back shed to cure in 1969.

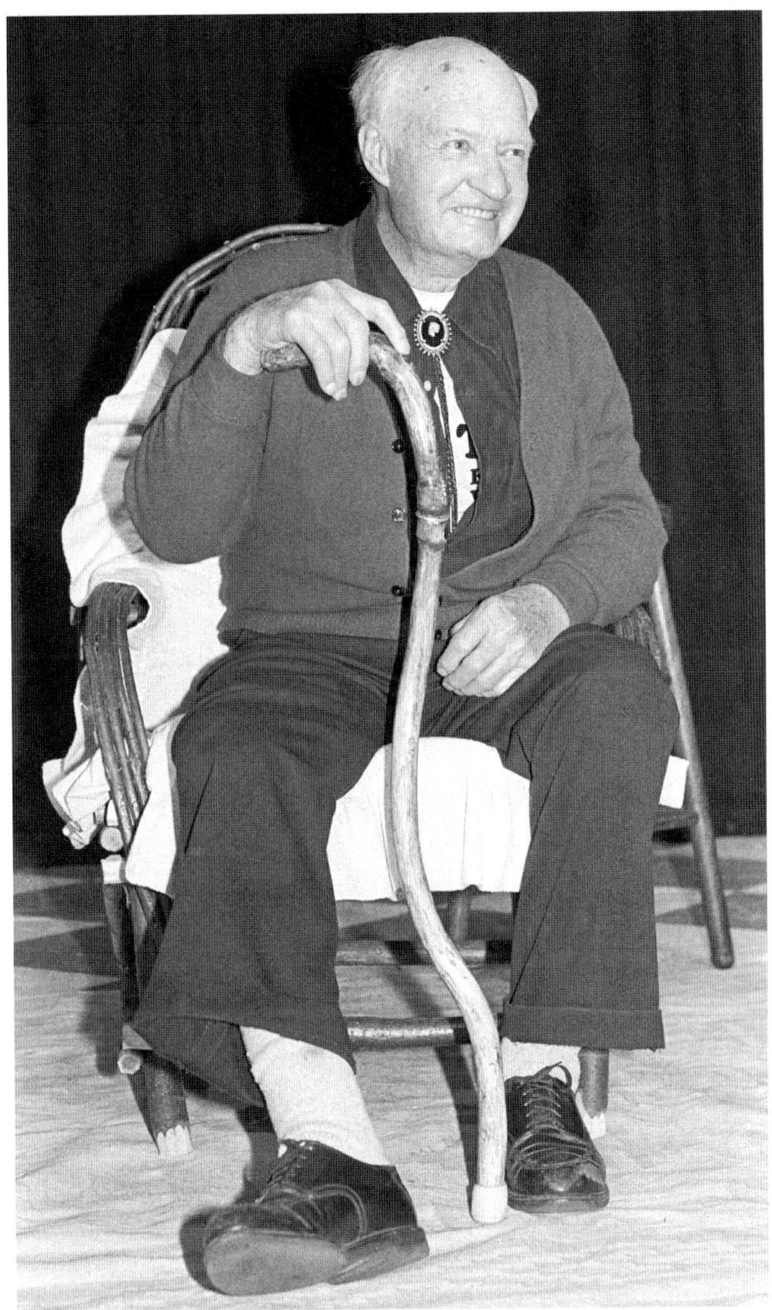

Frank Orazem's Walking Stick

Frank Orazem with his walking stick tells a story at Vinotok in 1986.

I FOUND THE KNOBBY BLONDE WALKING STICK, with the initials "F. O." inscribed on the top, in my mother's garage after her death. It had been a gift from its maker, Frank Orazem, more than twenty years earlier.

Frank Orazem was forever "seeing" figures in the pieces of wood that he collected near Horse Ranch Park over Kebler Pass. For his walking sticks, he favored wood with a natural curve. At home, he stripped the bark off and shellacked it. After inserting a metal washer in the bottom tip to keep it from wearing down, he marked it in black with his initials and presented the stick to a special friend.

One of those friends was Marcie Telander, with whom he collaborated on Vinotok. She took hers on stage, loaning it to many a nervous storyteller for use as a prop, in more than one sense of the word.

"It was a stick with a 'face' and large mouth, and he called it my 'story-telling staff.' He said I would 'carry our community's stories in the staff to other places and carry their stories back in the staff to share with our village,'" said Marcie. "His prediction was absolutely correct. I've done that for over twenty years."

Frank was adamant that his sticks not be called "canes."

"You don't have to be decrepit to be seen with one of these," he told me.

Frank could often be seen striding purposefully, walking stick in hand, down the street from his house on Elk Avenue near First Street to the bench at the Conoco where he passed the time with friends, or to the Catholic Church where he assisted the priest as a deacon. Deeply religious, he had once aspired to the priesthood. He drove older residents to Gunnison in his white sedan and paid regular visits to those who rarely left their homes because of poor health. He played a unique role in the community as both a caretaker of the elderly and a bridge to the younger, newer locals.

Nick Rayder became a local after moving to Crested Butte in the late 1980s. He volunteered to drive the Senior Van (a county-owned vehicle used to transport the elderly to Gunnison for doctors' appointments, shopping, and what not), and met Frank, a frequent user of the service, for the first time.

"We just bonded. I felt like he was my surrogate father. He told me, 'I don't know where you came from, but you are like a son to me,'" recalled Nick.

I enjoyed visiting Frank's home, which he had lived in since boyhood. It was more cluttered than my own, no mean feat. With his keen imagination, Frank crafted anything that struck his fancy, such as rocks and pieces of weathered wood, into knickknacks depicting humans or animals. He loved to pick up shiny things, uncovered by the melting snow, from the street—nails, bottlecaps, trinkets, coins—and he proudly displayed the "Junque Collage" he made with his found objects. Most impressive, he knew where everything that he

Charles W. Greenfield, 1969, alias "Chuck the Woodchuck," was Frank's fellow woodcrafter. He was born in Avery, Iowa, on March 8, 1906. He roamed the country as a jack-of-all-trades until 1936, when he arrived in Crested Butte and soon after married Francis Krizmanich. Chuck worked in the Big Mine until it closed in the 1950s, then hired on at the Gunnison County Road Department. After his retirement he spent his time woodworking in the garage behind his home until his death in 1988. He was a whiz at replacing the broken spindles of the old pressed back wooden chairs I was fond of refinishing. If he couldn't replace it with a spare he'd collected off a broken chair, he'd turn me a new one on his lathe.

ever collected could be found in his house, including his cigar box of 300 rubber bands. Each little knickknack came with a story, which Frank spun to his visitor.

Once when I came to play Scrabble with him and Nick Rayder, Frank took a wooden mallet and hit a mobile crafted of thin stones hanging from the ceiling. "That's rock music," he quipped. Nick and I groaned. And Frank proceeded to beat us soundly at Scrabble—almost every time.

The most delightful result of Frank's imagination was the heart he "saw" in a section of tree trunk. After sawing the arched wood down the middle to open it up, he placed the five-foot-tall sculptural heart in his back yard.

"He loved it when we brought the children from the preschool to visit his back yard and what we called 'Frank's Big Heart,'" recalled Marcie. A bachelor, he delighted in grand-fathering youngsters who didn't groan when he played his rock music.

Like many boys in Crested Butte he only attended school through the eighth grade before starting work in the mines. But he was an avid reader and formed a local book network. He passed his favorites to his friends living on White Rock Avenue: Michele Veltri, who shoveled Frank's snow, dropped the book by Charlie "Chuck the Woodchuck" Greenfield's. When he finished it, Chuck took it across the street to Nick, who returned it to Frank.

Frank's final morning, October 25, 1987, was spent in church lighting the candles for Mass. Grace Arnott, sitting up front, asked him, "How are you feeling this morning?" His reply: "I feel so bad, that if I could, I would lie down here and die." He collapsed just as Nick walked in the door.

Born in Leadville, Colorado, on December 17, 1907, he was two months shy of eighty. This rare, humble gentleman with the big heart is buried in the Crested Butte cemetery in a grave fittingly marked by that large wooden heart, moved from his back yard by Nick and his brother.

Nick inherited Frank's "Junque Collage" and his personal walking stick, although he surely has one of his own. I treasure my mother's awaiting me near the door of my garage, beckoning me to hike out and find my own treasures.

CHAPTER 22

Angie's Garden

Angelina (Angie) Oberosler, my gardening guru, in 1978. Born in Valdez, Colorado, Angie and her miner husband came to Crested Butte in 1949, where she quickly gained a reputation as an excellent cook and gardener. During the early 1960s she ran her Angelina's Laundry in the basement of the Company Store.

ANGIE OBEROSLER, my Elk Avenue neighbor, called me into her yard one day as I was hanging out laundry and pointed to a cardboard box filled with small droopy plants and clods of dirt.

"They're for you. I'm sick and tired of looking out my kitchen window and seeing that weedy, rocky slope in your backyard," she announced. "Plant them on your side hill, and I'll be able to see flowers when I'm cooking."

I duly accepted the gift of Icelandic poppy, columbine, and lupine plants, and the strawberry cuttings she had pruned from her flourishing garden. Even though I dug little holes for them, I had no faith. It was the first time in my life I had planted anything other than a sunflower seed in grade school. My only Crested Butte gardening experience had been sneaking over to Tony Lujan's garden after dark to steal strawberries with Henrietta Raines when we were seventeen.

Angie, in comparison, had both a prolific flower garden and a huge strawberry patch, from which she occasionally honored me with a bowl of luscious berries. Her youngest son, Frank, mowed their grass weekly and helped with the gardening chores.

The transplants started to perk up the next day, and a few weeks later actually blossomed. I went racing over to tell Angie. "They're growing, I mean, flowers and everything!" She nodded wisely. "You watch. It'll get better. They're perennials."

I went home and looked up perennials in the dictionary.

Later in the summer, I ran next door again. "Look, Angie! I got a strawberry!" I held it out proudly. She inspected it closely and handed it back. "Eat it," she said. "Tastes better than store bought, right?"

By the time I moved to my home on Sopris Avenue, I was brave enough to plant my own perennials from the seeds of those first plants. I rarely fertilized and accepted the frost and short growing season of the mountains, but I was thankful not to have the bugs and pests that plague low-elevation gardeners. That was before I saw my first slug. In late summer after the garden had grown enough to shade them from the hot sun, the slimy slugs, sporting a voracious appetite, shredded all my flowers nightly.

I turned to my gardening guru. "What am I going to do to get rid of the slugs? They're decimating the pansies."

"Oh, that's easy," Angie said. "Beer."

"Beer?"

"Sure. I just put a couple of dishes of beer in the garden each night. Frankie leaves me the backwash in his bottles after work. Slugs love beer. Once they crawl in, they can't get out and they drown."

ANGIE'S GARDEN

*Tony Lujan, 1980, was another gardening ace. In addition to cultivating a huge garden from which,
I am ashamed to admit, we stole strawberries, Tony was married to Susie, the best Mexican cook in town.*

I didn't drink beer. But I knew where to get a lot of half-empty cans of beer, fast. A couple of times a week, I crossed the road to the softball field. With a big paper bag in hand, I walked over to the players' bench.

"Hey guys, when you finish your beers, would you mind tossing them in this bag?"

"No problem."

After about three innings, I took my bag of beer cans and backwash and laid them around the garden on their sides.

The next morning, those sucker slugs were soused. "Gotta watch where you crawl in for a nightcap." I dumped them, coffins and all, into the trash. After I reported my success to Angie, she led me on a garden tour.

By then she was living up the block from me on Sopris Avenue in a large house Frank built in 1979 that had twice the garden as their old place. Because her varicose veins had worsened, she found it a strain to bend over or stand very long, so Frank did the dirt work and weeded the garden while Angie nurtured lilies, columbines, wildflowers, and other plants.

She walked heavily through her yard. "Look, this here's a gladiolus. I've been trying to get one of these to bloom for years. Summer is just too short."

"What's that one?" I pointed to a low shrub laden with large pink flowers.

"My peony. I think the hollyhocks will bloom in a week or so if we don't get any frost."

"My god, Angie, I've never even heard of those plants." I was outclassed, probably forever, and it must have showed on my face.

Then she shared her secret, a sinister sounding recipe for increasing the amount and beauty of flowers. The ingredients alone are enough to scare any plant into producing.

"Get yourself a gallon of warm water. Dissolve in it one teaspoon Epson salts, one half teaspoon ammonia, one teaspoon baking powder and one teaspoon saltpeter." She chuckled. "You should have seen the druggist the time I went in asking for saltpeter. I guess he thought I was dosing my husband to keep him out of my bed. Anyway, every two or three weeks, spray it on all your flowers. It'll keep off slugs . . . and mites, too."

She claimed her garden was so good-looking after a week of using the concoction that a florist wanted to buy her flowers on a regular basis.

"I lived at a lower altitude then, so I had a bit of an advantage. But," she cautioned, "never use it on your columbines."

I knew my garden would never rival Angie's, but I was proud of my double-ruffled orange Oriental poppies, which came from a seed packet I'd bought at Tony's Conoco and scattered carelessly. Several times I spied tourists photographing them. But I coveted the pink-blossomed variety and tried to grow them from seeds collected from plants around town. It was a dismal failure. I cried on Angie's shoulder. "I just can't make those seeds grow. I'm so frustrated."

"Sandy, why don't you just transplant that big pink plant from the west side of my old place on Elk Avenue," she suggested. "I bet the new owners will never miss it. Go in the fall. That's the best time."

     ANGIE'S GARDEN

*Every summer evening after chores were done, Angie Oberosler's neighbors,
Jessie Richardson and Marie Campbell, joined her on her porch, 1975.*

Frank Oberosler shoveling the roof of his mother's home on Elk Avenue in 1979.

I skulked over at dusk that September with my shovel and box and swiped the pink poppy before anyone saw me. I planted it under my picture window on the east side so I could look out and see it any time.

Lo and behold, the following spring after the snow melted it was growing green as could be. Late in the summer I raced up to Angie's.

"I've got five pink blossoms!"

"See, Sandy. You just have to be persistent at it."

The next summer, because of a drought it only yielded one bloom. The following year I didn't fertilize it, and by spring it seemed to have given up the ghost.

I never told Angie.

   ANGIE'S GARDEN

She had other things to deal with. She had checked herself into the Gunnison Health Care Center because she was now confined to a wheelchair. After emergency hernia surgery in 1993, she had no chance of returning home or ever gardening again.

In 1999 my husband and I built a new home in sagebrush acreage down valley, and we spent our first few summers pulling noxious weeds whose seeds had hitched a ride on contractors' trucks and heavy equipment. Our "garden" now is native grasses and wildflowers. But I cultivated a tiny patch near my office window of descendents from those first orange and yellow Icelandic poppies Angie gave me so many years ago. I finally grew my own Oriental poppy from seed—red instead of pink—and one of these days, I'm going to get up the nerve to ask the pharmacist for saltpeter.

CHAPTER 23

Ms. Grubstake 1980

Ms. Grubstake 1980 is overjoyed at the prospect of her $150 prize.

ENTER THE MS. GRUBSTAKE CONTEST. Swimsuit, Evening Gown, and Talent Categories. Judges' Questions. Win Fame, Fortune and $150 Cash!" That's the ad that bar owner Judy Naumburg placed in the local newspapers.

Well, shoot, I thought, she's just trying to make the place look respectable with a beauty contest. Hippies and young working guys were the usual patrons of the Grubstake Bar, not the old-timers or summer tourists. About once a week one of the boys hurled another—usually a friend or acquaintance—through the front plate-glass window. The perpetrator and victim were always three sheets to the wind, but duly paid Judy the cost of the glass. The Grubstake had changed a lot since the 1960s, when my family dined there. The $150 caught my fancy, though. I was paid a total of $40 a week—for three part-time jobs.

Beaucoup bucks in December 1979, $150 was the exact price of a plane ticket to Tucson, my Christmas vacation destination. And, I have to admit, like many women my age, I secretly dreamed of wearing a beauty queen crown on my head. I casually ran the idea past a few friends and got a variety of responses.

"You've got to be kidding!"

"Well, it could be a fun evening . . . I guess."

"Yes! Absolutely! You're a shoo-in!" Karen Austin fairly shouted at me. That clinched it. If the previous year's Ms. Grubstake thought I had a chance, then I was willing to give it a try.

"I'll do your makeup and loan you my false eyelashes, and we'll get Henrietta to do your hair."

I was a "sometimes lipstick with a little eyeliner and mascara" type. With the exception of Crested Butte Mountain Theatre productions, I didn't have the time or inclination to fool with curlers, foundation, powder, blush, and all that nonsense. *Crested Butte: where the guys are guys and the girls are, too* was the local joke. Both sexes dressed alike—jeans (usually ragged at the knees), boots, turtlenecks, sweaters, and ratty jackets in the winter. Since nearly everyone wore their hair long, it sometimes was tricky determining genders. Dresses and heels, not to mention pantyhose, had been tossed in an old suitcase in the back of the closet, the relics of an earlier life. With Karen in my court, though, anything was possible.

I figured I could handle the talent since I was a singer. Evening gown? No problem. My mother would loan me her blue sequined sheath. Swimsuit? Whoops. My lily-white winter body below a raccoon-eyed, ski-tanned face was not something I felt comfortable displaying in a bar full of leering eyes. My feet started getting cold. I confided my doubts to my sister Kathy.

"One hundred and fifty dollars. One hundred and fifty dollars." She chanted it like a mantra, and I joined in. I sure wasn't knock-down beautiful, and I'd never entered a beauty contest before, but the challenge—and the "fame and fortune"—won me over.

The Grubstake in 1975, before its awning collapsed from the weight of the snow.

Back at my closet I tried on my one and only bathing suit. A black-and-white number, the top and bottom were connected in the front by a narrow strip of material over my navel. Excluding a halter tie at my neck and a thin strap across my back, the rear view was of bare skin to my butt. Almost every part of me showed but my belly button and nonexistent cleavage. Tugging here and there, I rationalized: At least it matches my white skin. To complete my ensemble I'd wear my Lolita heart-shaped sunglasses.

The questions from the judges were not something for which I could prepare. I knew it would be a typical Crested Butte spoof on the Miss America contest. Not for us the inane, "Which person do you admire most in your life and why?" I did find out from Judy that the questions would be asked after the contestants traded swimsuits for evening gowns. What a relief to know I wouldn't be displaying a bare body in addition to a blank mind.

I worked hardest on the talent. For my song I chose "Second-Hand Rose." I rewrote the lyrics to parody my romantic history and plug the High Country Citizen's Alliance used clothing store, known as Saks Fourth Avenue. My costume consisted of a silly plumed hat, old-style handbag, bloomers, faded blouse, and gaudy jewelry.

Contest day arrived. Judy Naumburg covered the front windows of the bar with newspapers. There would be no hurlers, nor peepers, tonight. Admission was $20, and seating went fast; later arrivals had to stand all evening. A plywood "stage" and "runway" were built directly above the judges' table. They could have looked up our dresses. Not that they had to. The swimsuit competition, the big draw, would reveal our attributes or lack thereof.

     MS. GRUBSTAKE 1980

Some people were using the runway as a table, leaning on their elbows anticipating the big show.

We contestants—four of the bravest, or most stupid, women in town, depending on how you looked at it—were "backstage" in the restaurant side of the building. We'd each laid claim to a booth to use for our "dressing room." I shucked my jeans and started pulling on a pair of black stockings. Karen Austin snapped a photo of my newly sophisticated, false-eyelashed and blushed face, and bare thighs up to the crotch.

Pitchers of "root beer"—an alcoholic concoction popular at the time—started arriving. Although I can't for the life of me remember what was in them, they went down easy enough. It didn't take long to feel the liquor. We paraded out for our first waltz down the runway. A redheaded beauty, freestyle skiing champion Penelope Street, led the way. She had won international competitions performing graceful ballet-like moves on skis. It had not prepared her for spike heels. She tripped, nearly tumbling into the judges' laps. Tall, willowy Jade Davis, a Grubstake bartender and cocktail waitress, wore a slinky, full-length gown with her hair draped sexily over one eye. I had her figured as the local favorite and probable winner.

Judy wisely stationed a "stage manager" to help us down the stairs of the plywood stage and through the cramped liquor storage area and kitchen to our booths. As the evening progressed we needed his steady arm more and more.

I was getting tipsy. Heck, we all were. That was the idea, I guess. I put on the brakes. Bad enough to be half undressed in front of everyone. Why compound it by getting falling-down—literally—drunk as well? I was the only one who made that decision . . . and those pitchers of root beer kept on coming . . . and coming.

By the arrival of the swimsuit competition, Jade's sexy eyes had started to droop; she reminded me of a tall iris bloom wilting in the sun. She was so relaxed she couldn't speak. Gorgeous Penelope was listing left during the swimsuit competition. Her skimpy suit covered up all the vitals, but with strings across her ribs tying the front and back pieces together, she still exposed more—and whiter—skin than I did. I didn't know the other contestant, who went only by the name of Jules. Rumor later had it she left town the following week. Her overflowing bosom put all of ours to shame, and her bikini left nothing to the imagination. She too, started looking foolish in her inebriation. Wondering if I looked like a penguin in my swimsuit, I handed a tube of suntan lotion to a guy ogling up from the edge of the runway and invited him to apply it to my back, eliciting whistles and catcalls.

I'm not sure anyone remembers the talent portion of the contest. I came across the words to my song twenty years later, and I have a photograph of my performance in that silly costume. Surely I sang on key. And I heard laughter at my lyrics. The root beers must have had an effect after all—on *all* of us there.

We changed back into our evening gowns, and the judges, including Judy Naumburg, Lee Ervin (editor of the *Crested Butte Pilot*), and Mayor W Mitchell, started asking the questions. Judy slowly and distinctly read the only one I can remember.

"If you were giving _______ a (sexual act), where would you start?"

"The penguin" in the swimsuit competition, 1979.

The crowd whooped and hollered at his name. Crested Butte is such a small town that everyone knew this conservative, totally straight older guy who, as far as could be determined, had never dated or slept with anyone, smoked pot or cigarettes or gotten drunk. He was, in short, a Crested Butte version of a nerd. You can bet he was not in the audience that night.

"At his head," I replied. Meaning inside his brain. My inadvertent double entendre went right over *my* head, but not the crowd's. The audience went wild.

After some deliberation by the judges, Karen Austin swept out onto the stage and placed the rhinestone tiara on my head. She took off her red full-length cape with a tinseled edge and draped it around my shoulders, pinning a red satin ribbon across my chest proclaiming "Ms. Grubstake 1980" in black magic marker. My fill-in photographer, Dick Meyer, snapped my beaming face for posterity and for the *Crested Butte Chronicle.* Judy handed me a dozen red roses, and I took my victory promenade down the runway. Suddenly it was no longer plywood. I was a glamorous beauty queen, my tiara was diamond, and my $150 prize seemed a king's ransom.

Judy brought me back to earth by later confiding that she'd traveled all the way to Grand Junction, a three-hour drive, to find the rhinestone tiara at the five-and-dime store. It and my sash held a place of honor on my bedroom dresser mirror for years, although the tiara broke and had to be wired together for the following summer's July Fourth parade.

Later I posed for a shot lying full length across the stage, and when asked the secret to my success by *Chronicle* reporter Paul Andersen, I replied without hesitation. "I stayed sober."

Mary Yelenick, the Weather Woman

Mary Yelenick in her Crested Butte Liquor Store on Elk Avenue in 1980.

MARY YELENICK'S THIRD GRADERS used to vie for the privilege of walking under her "wings." She held her arms out like a big bird, and a child would cuddle up under each side as they paraded to the post office during lunch.

Mary taught school for thirty years, and every person she met was someone to be cuddled and cared for. She became a town confidante, due as much to the location of her and husband Frank's liquor store across the street from the old post office at 314 Elk Avenue (now the Rocky Mountain Chocolate Factory) as to her patience and curiosity. Mary knew who was having a birthday, who was visiting whom, and who was in the hospital. She always sent a card to the ailing friend, enclosing a dollar bill. Sweeping the sidewalk in front of their store every morning, she took time to chat with everyone passing by. In the 1960s and 1970s, not too many people were passing by, so she had leisurely conversations with each one.

For renters like myself, the Crested Butte Liquor Store was a veritable treasure trove of empty boxes. In the days before recycling, when moving time came, I paid a visit to the liquor store and Mary just kept bringing them out from the back room, while I packed them into my Toyota.

BORN IN CRESTED BUTTE on September 28, 1903, Mary Tezak earned her degree from Western State College in Gunnison "in snitches and snatches," because there was no on-campus housing and commuting was difficult.

She began her teaching career in 1923 in Baldwin (a now-deserted mining camp near Ohio Pass) as one of two teachers, instructing thirty students in grades one through four. In 1925–1926 she taught all eight grades in Almont and still found time to marry Frank Yelenick. At the end of the 1926 school year, the newlyweds purchased their 307 Elk Avenue building (built in 1898) from a couple named Murphy and opened the Western Hotel. Mary ran a restaurant on one side of the building, and they raised their daughter, Genevieve, and son, Joseph "Bud", in their apartment on the other side. Frank, a Yugoslavian immigrant, worked at the Smith Hill Mine.

In 1932, after their children were old enough to start school, Mary returned to teaching the elementary grades at the Crested Butte school. She would often stay late to teach home economics to the junior and senior high school girls. When she retired in 1969, her replacement was a former pupil, Nettie Kapushion, who noted ruefully, "I walked in and she walked out, although she did return temporarily when enrollment went up."

Nettie had been one of the children who found comfort under her former teacher's "wings." She remembers a particular home economics class where "we cooked a three-course meal in the old kitchen [of the former high school at Maroon Avenue and Fifth Street] for all the school board members, and served them in the gym."

In 1947 Frank quit mining and they opened a liquor store in their former restaurant. Dropping in for a bottle, I could often smell the evening meal in their apartment next door. A bell on the door announced a customer, and Mary would appear wearing a hairnet, and an apron over her dress. I never saw her in pants. The wine selection was a bit skimpy, but they always had Coors and Budweiser beer, and basic hard liquor on the back shelves—gin, vodka, rum, and whiskey. Nothing fancy, but it did the job.

Eternally polite and gracious, Mary always asked about my health and listened to my problems, even if I was interrupting her dinner while I made my selection. She sent me on my way with, "Do tell your mother hello for me." I think because her daughter's name was Genevieve, like my mother's, she felt a connection. A friend once said, "I never saw Mary in a bad mood." Tired, sick, and stubborn, but rarely grumpy.

During warm summer days, Frank sat out front on an up-ended wooden Pepsi crate. A quiet man, he spoke with a Slavic accent, like many of his contemporaries. Jeanne La-Tourette Gifford, relatively new to Crested Butte, freely entrusted her infant into Frank's large, work-worn hands while she made her purchases inside. He would beam a toothless smile below the dark glasses he always wore following his cataract surgery.

Because money was scarce, Mary held several part-time jobs. Putting her knowledge of her neighbors' comings and goings to good use, she wrote a column for the *Crested Butte Chronicle* (long before I arrived in 1964) entitled, "Getting Around." In addition to all the paper work at the liquor store, she was a notary public, and she volunteered as the secretary for St. Joseph's, a local fraternal order.

Mary was also Crested Butte's official weather woman. Each Wednesday, I called her to get the week's highs, lows, and rain or snow accumulations to print in the *Crested Butte Pilot,* and then asked, "Have you got any tidbits for Rambling Babs?" I knew that with a little coaxing she could add a couple of inches to my social column, and I was never disappointed. To her credit, she never divulged anything that couldn't be printed.

When I asked how she got the job as weather woman, she explained that her cousin Jane Plutt, who formerly held the position, had moved to Grand Junction in 1951 with her husband, after the mine where he was employed closed. Mary agreed to take over the job in Jane's name, just in case the Plutts returned to Crested Butte. They never did, so for twenty-one years she earned all of $3.50 a month for climbing two flights of stairs daily in the back of the liquor store to read the instruments and report the temperatures and precipitation to her "employer," the U.S. Department of Commerce. She quit in 1976, "only because of my health." Years on her feet had taken their toll on her legs.

In 1985 illness forced the Yelenicks to close the store they had owned for thirty-eight years and move to the Gunnison Health Care Center. Mary died shortly thereafter, on November 21, 1985, at age eighty-two.

In the months following Mary's death, the seeds were sown to make Mary's "wings" permanent. Myles Rademan, Crested Butte planner, presented a proposal to the town council: a park built not by taxes, but by the efforts of the whole community—from drawing board to playground. As a tribute to the gentle former schoolteacher, who so loved children and

Frank Yelenick holds Molly Gifford in 1980.

was affectionately known as "everybody's grandmother," it would be called the "Mary Yelenick Playground." We had named the adjoining softball field after old-timer and umpire Pitsker Sporcich. It seemed only fitting that a children's playground bear Mary's name.

Six months of planning and fundraising ensued. The park was financed with dog fines, baby beauty contests, and daffodil, T-shirt, and bake sale donations. Contractors donated equipment, sand for the sandbox, and lumber for the jungle gym. Cash and volunteers came out of the woodwork.

More than 100 residents spent the weekend of June 21 and 22, 1986, sawing, sanding, and installing—whatever it took—to erect playground equipment. Much like an old-fashioned barn raising, each person contributed his or her skills. In addition, lunches were organized, daycare was arranged, and there was even a "quartermaster" to keep track of all the donated tools. When the Sunday-night barbecue rolled around at the end of forty-eight hours, we had a new park with swings, sandboxes, a rope climb, monkey bars, a spiral slide, a tire swing, and other climbing apparatus.

"The town that built a park" was even featured on statewide television.

On the July Fourth weekend of 1986, the playground was formally dedicated. A frail Frank Yelenick, attired in his best black suit and hat, was led by his son to the bronze plaque atop a wooden base with its heartfelt inscription: "Mary Yelenick Playground, dedicated with fond memories to Mary Yelenick, September 28, 1903—November 21, 1985. Beloved by family, friends, and children. The labors and donations of the people of Crested Butte have made this park a place for all to enjoy."

Over the ensuing twenty years, some of the playground equipment has been replaced. The children for whom it was built are approaching adulthood and leaving the nest. I, however, returned to stay in Crested Butte, heeding Mary's final admonition to me in 1983 when I stopped in for boxes on my way to a year of acting school in California: "you come back, dear; you're one of us now." I think I know how those children under her wings must have felt.

CHAPTER 25

Buried in Paradise

Looking up Paradise Divide from the Crested Butte cemetery in 1975, carpeted with daisies.

I BEGAN WANDERING among the graves, picking daisies, in the Crested Butte cemetery in 1965. It was my first visit to any cemetery, so I didn't find it odd that the tall white daisies grew wild among the sagebrush, or that only a cattle guard marked the entrance, and barbed wire fenced out the cows grazing nearby.

The cemetery is on the ski area road, past the old town dump on a knoll overlooking the Slate River. It has an unobstructed view toward town on the south, Paradise Divide on the west, Crested Butte Mountain on the east, and the ski area to the north. It's a lovely place for a home. And in a way it is—housing bones and ashes, memories, and history. We like to make the body's burial site a special place. We decorate it, revere it, and visit it, which means that graves are mostly for the living.

A meander through the Crested Butte cemetery is like thumbing through a history book or climbing a family tree. On either side of the narrow dirt road to the small chapel are grave lots bordered with concrete footers and antique iron fences. Many of the names inscribed on the white marble monuments belong to families whose names you'll still find in the Crested Butte and Gunnison phone books. In the 1960s I knew only a few people. Today my friends and acquaintances number in the hundreds, and too many of them lie there. Every June, I pay them a visit.

There's Tony Kapushion up on the hill, where he's got a view of his ranch. Ski area founder Dick Eflin likes to tell the story of how he commented to Tony over a beer at Tony's Tavern, "God, it's pretty here." Tony's dry reply as he collected Dick's dime for the beer: "Yep, but you can't eat scenery." I roomed with Nettie, Tony's daughter, at the University of Colorado. Today she lives in her grandfather's homestead cabin on the Washington Gulch Road. She and her first husband, Jim Sweeney, who proposed to her over dinner at my house, renovated the tumbledown one-room shell into a cozy home in the 1970s. Jim now lies near Tony in the Kapushion lot, as does Nettie's second husband, Fred Dyer.

At the other end of the fifteen-acre cemetery is the Kochevar lot. Fritz Kochevar, whose mother grew citrus trees from seed inside the front of what today is Kochevar's Saloon on Elk Avenue, taught me how to shoot pool. In 1973 he joined his brothers and sisters in the family plot.

And at the very highest point is John and Frances Somrak's lot. John used to joke about "homesteading" their lot, taken with the idea that, like the owners of today's trophy homes, he would have a fantastic view.

"I could see town, the road to the ski area, and people fishing in the Slate River." And now he does.

In the summer of 1987, Crested Butte town clerk Kerry Folger, who shared my fascination with the cemetery, concentrated on a long overdue task—bringing the cemetery map and master list of gravesites and occupants up to date.

The Kapushion homestead cabin in 1969 before its renovation. Today it is surrounded by subdivisions.

"The cemetery is my pet project," she told me. I could imagine her badgering the town council and mayor to permit her to shuck most of her duties at the Town Hall office and spend a couple of weeks strolling among the daisies and gravestones, clipboard, notebook, and map in hand, documenting all the burial sites. The weeks turned into the entire summer, and Kerry's mother, Betty Fischer, here for her annual summer visit, served as Kerry's assistant. Once the word got out, information started trickling in.

"Hazel Gardiner, whose sister Berneice retired as the town postmistress in the 1960s and is buried here, wrote to say that years ago it was named the 'Fairview Cemetery,'" said Kerry. "And I've discovered that the most common surname in the cemetery is Kochevar, with nineteen graves. Other plentiful names are Kapushion, Chiodo, Gallowich, Gardiner, Kerr, and Kvaternick."

Kerry explained that the cemetery is laid out very much like the town. There are sixty-seven blocks with sixteen lots to a block. According to Kerry's completed record in 1987, there were 852 occupied or reserved sites in the cemetery. Four blocks of gravesites had been set aside for the burial of paupers. No one was buried there as far as Kerry could determine.

Angelo Chiodo, in 1969, was uncle to June Krizmanich.
A retired miner and former member of the Gunnison County road crew, he had a few blocks
further than Fritz Kochevar to drive to the bars, but managed to do it more slowly.

But when I talked to C. J. Miller, owner of Miller's Funeral Home in Gunnison, he said, "Sometimes it's hard to tell if there's a grave. The rain and snow smooths the land over after years."

Kerry also discovered 320 names that were not recorded on the town's master burial list. Her theory was that previous town officials didn't keep track of who was actually buried there, so the list of names didn't correspond with the names of those who had purchased lots. C. J. Miller theorized that the discrepancy might be explained by the presence of another funeral home in the county years ago.

"When it went out of business, it could have lost some of the records."

His own funeral home, a family operation started by his great-grandfather Adam Miller from Pennsylvania, was based in Gunnison. A Crested Butte branch was located at 201 Elk Avenue. But its records go back only to 1929.

"It's the duty of the town, not the funeral home, to maintain the records," he said. "Many people used to embalm the body in their own homes," he added.

But usually when they needed the undertaker, they turned to the Miller Funeral Home.

"My grandmother Susie Julian Miller was the tough one. One time right after she had had her teeth pulled and bridges put in, she was called to our Crested Butte mortuary. A special train was hooked up—it was in the winter—and she went up from Gunnison to embalm twelve men who had been killed in a mine accident."

C. J. also told us that fifty-four of the sixty miners killed in the Jokerville Mine explosion of January 24, 1884, were buried in a mass grave, which old-timer Rudy Sedmak thought is under two tombstones just north of the main entrance in the oldest section of the cemetery. An iron monument incorporating a gold pan and railroad spike was crafted by Jim Wallace in the 1970s and placed near the mass grave as a tribute to these victims. Its inscription reads, "Their lives were gentle and the elements so mixed in them that nature might stand up and say to all the world they were men."

The mass grave is not indicated in the town records, but Kerry said that six lots contain unmarked graves, and there are also marked graves placed outside the borders of their lots. In other words, it's all a bit vague in spots, but what do you expect after 153 years?

Although tales abound of not being able to bury the dead in the winter because of the frozen ground, C. J. dispelled that myth.

"Actually the ground is easy to dig because the snow acts as an insulator. We have, however, had to carry a casket quite a ways through deep snow to the grave, and there have been times when it's been really hard to see because of a snowstorm."

Snow often stopped the train from Gunnison and, according to C. J., when the train could only get as far as Cement Creek, his grandmother Susie traveled on foot the rest of the way to the funeral parlor in Crested Butte.

In the old days, mourners had wakes and walked to the cemetery. The town, always short on funds after the last mine closed in 1952, only plowed snow when necessary. It sometimes took two or three days for a backhoe operator to make his way in through a winter's worth of snow, which could be as deep as six feet.

In 1987 a burial lot could be purchased for $50. The 22-foot by 11-foot space can hold between six and eight people, depending on the size of the deceased, and if he/she is cremated or buried in a coffin. However, the Karolina and Jacob Kochevar lot contains ten graves, because most of them are for babies. Kerry remembered a run on cemetery lots in the late 1980s, when many young people took advantage of the price, joking, "It's the best real estate deal in town." It was the cheapest price in the state as well.

During that time I visited the town offices and found Kerry laughing with her co-workers. On the floor were lines of masking tape.

"What's the big joke?" I asked.

Town manager Bill Crank interrupted his peals of laughter. "An older woman who has lived here all her life came in to talk to Kerry about buying two cemetery lots. Kerry told her you could put seven people in each one. The lady vehemently disagreed, and from my office across the hall I could hear the conversation getting more heated. The lady left and said she'd be back after lunch to pick out the lots on the map.

"The town hall meeting room is fifteen by twenty-four feet. Kerry got building inspector Fred Dyer to measure out eleven by twenty-two feet on the floor, which they marked with masking tape. During lunch Kerry gathered up the town staff. When the lady arrived to pay for her lot, someone ushered her into the conference room. There we were, seven of us including Kerry, flat on our backs inside the "lot," shoulder-to-shoulder, with our eyes closed and hands crossed over our chests. We broke out laughing at the absurdity of it, and at first I think she thought we were laughing at her. Later on, though, she got a chuckle out of it."

As Crested Butte grew, immigrants from different nationalities loosely congregated. Old-timer Matt Volk drew me a map once as we drank a beer in Frank and Gal's Bar. The Italians settled on White Rock Avenue; Croatians near Elk Avenue and Second Street; the Slovenians in the northeast section; and the Irish, German, and English folks near the Union Congregational Church. When the Colorado Fuel and Iron Company brought in a group of miners to run the Big Mine, it built an 1880s version of tract homes on Big Mine Hill. Mexicans occupied many of the drafty two-bedroom houses, and when the mines closed some of the shacks were moved to Gunnison.

The cemetery was divided in much the same way, according to Frances Somrak, long-time resident.

"People stuck together when they lived together. It was the same in death. The Croatians, Slovenians, and Italians are in a different section than the Irish, German, and English." Of course, intermarriage over the years skewed that a bit, I noted. And Frances laughed in agreement.

"My husband John and I were one of each—Croatian and Slovenian."

I was told years ago that the Catholics are mostly buried near St. Patrick's Chapel. A modest brown wooden building of about 250 square feet, the chapel sits near the high point

Matt Volk in 1980. Baby bottle in his pocket, he was looking after his granddaughter when I shot his photograph.

*Ralph Falsetto in 1968. His family—of Italian descent—
lived on White Rock Avenue, just as Matt Volk explained.*

Frances Somrak in her kitchen in 1974.

of the cemetery. Were it not for a simple cross at the roof peak, you might mistake it for a maintenance shed. The interior, however, is a work of art. The ornate altar is graced with finely carved statues of Jesus, Joseph holding the baby Jesus, the Virgin Mary, and, at the very top, the Pope brandishing a shamrock. To one side is a crèche with shepherds and lambs. A stenciled inscription across the bottom reads "Donated by St. Mary's Society." A painting of Mary gazes benevolently from the south wall.

Before they moved to Gunnison, June and John Krizmanich were the chapel caretakers. They cleaned it before Memorial Day and in the autumn nailed boards over the large windows to protect them from the snow.

"Who does the chapel key belong to?" I asked.

"Why, it belongs to all of us!" exclaimed June.

And she is right. The whole town built the chapel, which was dedicated on September 2, 1963. On the wall near the altar are two typewritten lists containing three hundred names of financial contributors and thirty-three of those who donated labor and materials (including many names from Gunnison). Bill Lacy Sr., who ranched just south of Crested Butte, was the crew foreman. Donations ranged from $1 to $110. Most were in the $5 range.

"Back then, $5 to us was like $500 now," said June.

It is beyond the chapel where the real history lies. Resting beneath the stones and crosses surrounding the chapel are early settlers, including (legend has it) a Grand Dragon in the Ku Klux Klan. The oldest marked grave is that of Rosie Haeck, who was born and died on the same day in 1851. There are many markers for babies, firebricks surrounding one small grave and pink quartz stones bordering another. These babies lived only days, months, or perhaps a couple of years before succumbing to diseases against which today's infants are routinely vaccinated.

Many folks died in early adulthood. A few committed suicide, although you'd never know it from the inscription. My neighbor Lyle McNeill told me that it was customary to bury such people in the opposite direction of the neighboring graves. Most graves face east, so a suicide would be buried with the head toward the west.

The monuments are handcrafted of a variety of materials: pink Italian marble, white marble—from the quarry at the nearby town of Marble—sandstone, granite, rock, metal, and wood. Some of the ornate lettering on the older stones is overgrown with lichen. Many monument inscriptions are religious; others are from poems or literature. All are heartfelt.

"Beloved, how we miss you" for Guss Schaefer. "She loved People" for Lucy J. Marasco. "Life is hard but living is great. We lived in these mountains" for Dr. and Mrs. A. O. Singleton, a couple from Texas who spent vacations at their ski area home with their twin daughters and son. Decorated with musical notes, "Headed down the wrong highway" for George A. Spritzer. A short sandstone cross crudely marks Gilbert Garcia's grave; he died the day he was born in 1919. One child's gravestone is inscribed, "Gone to be an angel."

A local councilman and longtime resident who purchased a gravesite on the east side of the chapel, facing Crested Butte Mountain, once said, "I plan to have inscribed on my gravestone, 'Hope you like the view, I can't see a thing.'"

An angel watches over a young one's grave. Crested Butte Mountain guards them both.

Rose Tezak's grave marker in 1987 holds a photograph of the young girl, who died in 1935 at age twelve.

Mementos are also placed on graves, disturbed only by the weather. A ceramic flower vase crafted by his brother Tom sits next to the marker of Doug Ayraud. Tree stumps support a nearby bench made of wooden planks. I once found "I love you, Daddy" written with tiny rocks on the fresh mounded earth covering a murdered father.

Several of the grave markers sport photographs. The Stajduhar family gravestone has one of the couple: Gregory, 1884–1963, and Catherine, 1889–1958. A photo of a baby in her cradle is affixed to another monument.

No one seems sure of the exact process. C. J. Miller speculated the photographs were sent to the monument company and coated with epoxy material to keep them from fading in the morning sun. It's possible the emulsion is transferred onto porcelain. The tradition is very Eastern European. I check them out each summer to see if they have faded. I was crushed one Memorial Day to discover that the photo of Frances Sneler, 1873–1941 [Tom Snellar's mother], had been gouged out of the stone. (Translations of names from Croatian have changed over generations.)

Sagebrush grows as high as the monuments in some places, but that doesn't prevent the families from rooting it out and covering the grave in their choice of material—white gravel, raked dirt, roses, columbines, wildflowers, pine trees, aspen, or shrubs. Many

BURIED IN PARADISE

graves are adorned with faded plastic flowers or miniature American flags in glass bottles and jars, which are washed and rearranged for the traditional cemetery visit during the Memorial Day Mass at the chapel.

A cemetery fund was started in 1987, and June Krizmanich suggested it be used to clear the sagebrush from the walkways so that older people could walk more easily among the graves. In May 1988 some of the money was spent erecting an ornate iron arch on rock pedestals at the entrance reading "Crested Butte Cemetery." Despite its accuracy, the "Fairview" name was relegated to the past. Several trees were planted near the arch.

"I remember going out every day one summer to hand-water those damn trees at the entrance when they were first planted," Kerry said. She still laughs about it fifteen years later. But the trees, transplanted from John and Frances Somrak's property on Elk Avenue, thrived due to Kerry's loving attention and/or the New Age crystals she planted with their rootballs. An underground sprinkler system was installed to water the newly planted lawn and aspen trees by the chapel. June's suggestion fell by the wayside, and most of the sagebrush remains.

Kerry was convinced that upgrading the cemetery would add to the town's summer tourist trade.

"We've got a lot of people coming here to research family names. When I was mapping the cemetery I saw at least two cars a day stop by."

Back in the early 1960s, however, the cemetery as a tourist site was the farthest from anyone's mind. To the local teens it was "the boonies," their favorite parking spot—especially in the winters before the dirt road was plowed to the new ski area. Today busloads of skiers pass the cemetery every fifteen minutes, and tourists gaze out the windows as uncaring about the history buried under the snow as were the lusty, local teens of the 1960s.

THE CEMETERY FEELS MUCH THE SAME as it did in 1965—sagebrush still tears at your ankles, and weathered picket and iron fences sag a bit more from each year's snow. The white oxeye daisies that I used to love are now officially listed by the state as noxious weeds. The "fair view" is as beautiful as ever. Under the ground or above it, you're still in Paradise. And for all we know, Tony Kapushion is finally at leisure to feast his eyes on his beloved land, "eating scenery."

In 1988 a wrought iron arch was erected at the cemetery entrance, paid for with donations.

According to the Croatian inscription, these babies died in infancy.
A photo of one is inlaid in the marble, 1987.

These cows got sidetracked at the cemetery in 1988. The chapel is in the background.